The Road to Austerlitz

The Road to Austerlitz

Napoleon's Campaign
of 1805

R. G. Burton

The Road to Austerlitz
by R. G. Burton

First published under the title
From Boulogne to Austerlitz
1912

Leonaur is an imprint
of Oakpast Ltd

Copyright in this form © 2008 Oakpast Ltd

ISBN: 978-1-84677-582-6 (hardcover)
ISBN: 978-1-84677-581-9 (softcover)

http://www.leonaur.com

Publisher's Notes

In the interests of authenticity, the spellings, grammar and place names used have been retained from the original editions.

The opinions of the authors represent a view of events in which he was a participant related from his own perspective, as such the text is relevant as an historical document.

The views expressed in this book are not necessarily those of the publisher.

Contents

Europe in 1804–1805	9
Character of the Opposing Forces	18
Advance to the Rhine	29
From the Rhine to Ulm	42
From Ulm to Austerlitz	55
Operations in Italy and the Tyrol	74
The Battle of Austerlitz	79
The Causes of Success	100
An Overview of the Campaign	107

All great nations learned their truth of words and strength of thought in war; they were nourished in war and wasted by peace; taught by war and deceived by peace; trained by war and betrayed by peace; in a word, they are born in war and expired in peace.
Ruskin.

CHAPTER 1

Europe in 1804–1805

In sketching the events which led up to the campaign of Austerlitz, in 1805, it is necessary to go back to May 1803, when the Peace of Amiens came to an end. That peace could probably in no case have remained lasting. The continued occupation of Malta and Alexandria by England; the toleration of a scurrilous press, directed against the First Consul, in London; the British naval preparations—all these were calculated to arouse the hostility of Napoleon, while territorial acquisitions by France in Genoa and Piedmont, and the character of the First Consul himself, were not factors which made for the maintenance of peace.

The renewal of hostilities with England marked the initiation of Napoleon's project for the invasion of that country; for this purpose the Grand Army was assembled on the shores of the Channel, England and a corps under Bernadotte was stationed in Holland. In July 1803 the First Consul established his famous "Continental System" for the exclusion of British trade from the continent of Europe; in March 1804 the seizure and execution of the Duc d'Enghien aroused horror and indignation of all the dynasties of the Continent.

In May, Napoleon was crowned Emperor of the French, thus consolidating his military and political power in the state. He had now at length supreme authority, both to direct policy and to organise the means to carry it into effect. By July he had assembled a numerous and well-equipped army for the invasion of England, and his troops in camp at Boulogne swore allegiance to the newly made Emperor, who was seated in the iron chair of Dagobert, in the midst of his vast camp, from whence in the misty distance he could discern, in imagination if not in reality, those white cliffs of Albion which marked the goal of his ambitions. From Boulogne he proceeded to Aachen, the ancient capital of Charlemagne, his predecessor in the Empire of the West a thousand years before.

Nothing but the humbling of England appeared wanting to the triumph of his genius and ambition, and to the establishment of almost illimitable power. "Masters of the Channel for six hours, we are masters of the world," wrote the Emperor, and there appears to be little doubt that his intention of invading England was real, although many historians have averred the contrary. Certainly, the preparations for a descent were equally efficacious for carrying on a Continental war, which, according to many, was the intention he cloaked under his scheme of invasion. In pursuance of this scheme he had assembled an army of 150,000 men on the shores of the Channel, and had collected a large number of flat-bottomed boats and other transports to convey them to the English coast. The French coast was fortified against English attacks, and every preparation was made for the expedition, down to the smallest detail.

The clearance of the Channel or the absence of the English fleet was all that was wanted for the project to be put into execution; and for this purpose Napoleon had organised a great fleet, at first under command of Latouche Tréville, and subsequently under Villeneuve. This squadron was to draw off the English fleet to the West Indies, while a second squadron, under Gauteaume, which was in Brest harbour, would convey Augereau's division to Ireland.

Napoleon considered that he would be able to destroy the shipyards of Plymouth and Portsmouth, and enter London in three weeks, there to dictate terms of peace. In Ireland he would find a disloyal population eager to welcome any enemies of England, and ready to raise the flag of revolution. It is recorded

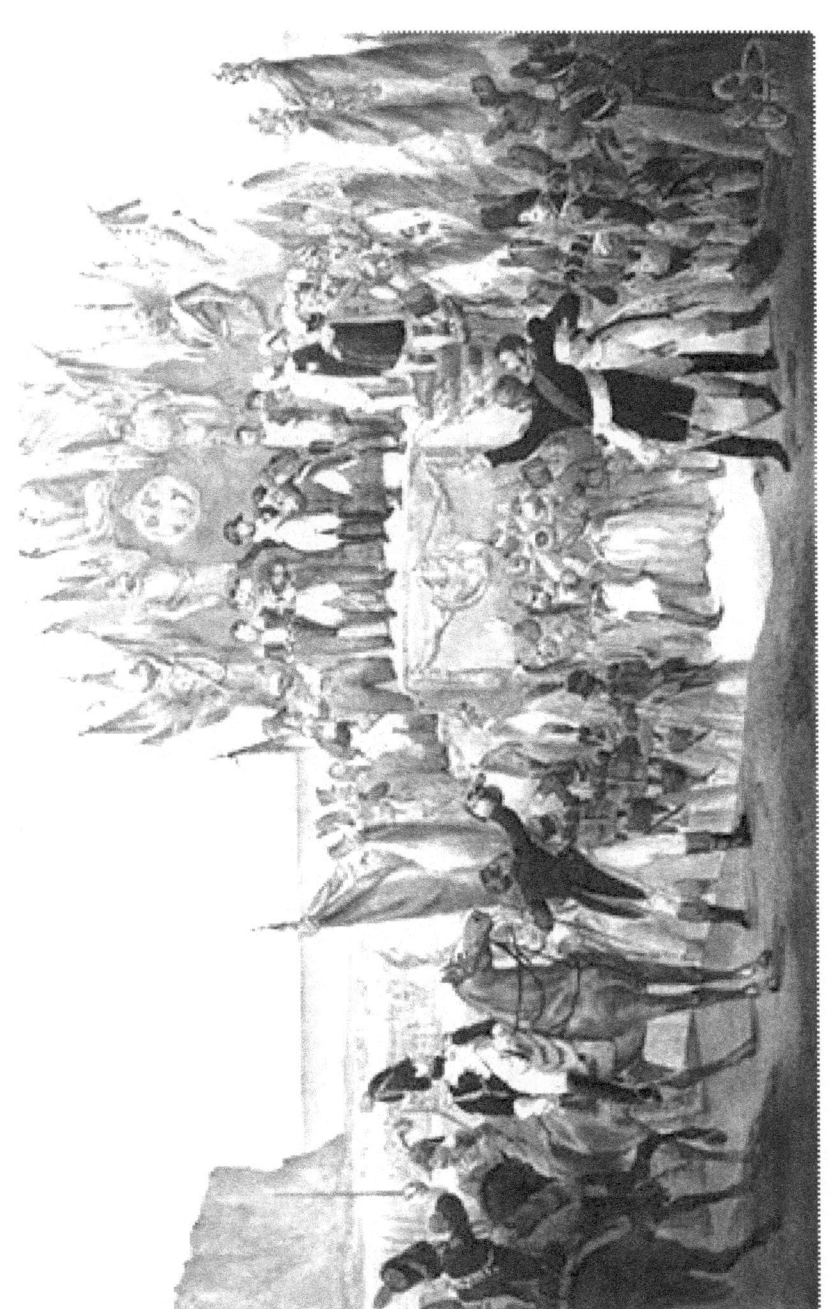

legion-d'honneur

that an Irish exile named O'Connor, a general of division in Augereau's army, had several interviews with Napoleon in May 1805, and endeavoured to persuade him that the best way to conquer England was to go first to Ireland.

It was agreed that all the English in Ireland should be exterminated. That the danger in Ireland was real is shown by the events of 1798, when a raiding party of 1000 landed in that country without opposition after a sixteen days' voyage, having escaped the observation of the English navy. Four times they defeated British forces opposed to them; captured eleven guns, and for nearly three weeks engaged the attention of all the troops in Ireland, some 10,000 men. Napoleon was not the last to entertain ideas as to the feasibility of the invasion of England; and in this connection, and to throw some light on the views of the General Staff in Berlin, the following passage from the work of the late Count Yorck von Wartenburg [1] is of considerable interest:—

> The fact that this landing was not effected, and England not conquered, is generally considered by historians as the salvation of Europe, for one country at least escaped Napoleon's domination. I do not share this opinion. The States of the Continent suffered at the time too severely and directly from Napoleon's tyranny for them to realise that England had not less exclusively, though in a more

---

1. *Napoleon as a General.* By Count Yorck von Wartenburg (Kegan Paul, Trench, Trübner & Co.). "This plan shows his genius at its full height. The idea which underlay his landing was perfectly correct; it was a putting into practice of the highest rules of war, namely, 'try to put your strong points as to time and space against the enemy's weak points.' Napoleon's strength lay in his army and war on land; England's strength consisted in its fleet and in war at sea; to attack her in such a way that his strength might be brought to bear was, therefore, assuredly good strategy. Napoleon has been condemned because the execution of his plan is said to have been impossible. But if we remember all that has been declared impossible in the history of the world by contemporaries, and yet was achieved by the power of genius, who can say that a landing of his army in England would have been an impossibility for Napoleon? Hannibal's great plan of crossing the Alps and attacking Rome in Italy and conquering it there, would perhaps have been considered impossible now had it remained a plan only.

practical and enduring manner, its own interests in view, and by no means those of Europe at that time. Had Napoleon entered England at the head of his army, his strength would on the one hand have been weakened thereby, and the Continent would have obtained greater freedom of action, and on the other hand England, shaken to its very foundations at home, would not have been able to concentrate, as it did, almost the whole colonial possessions of the world in its own hands, and the Continental powers would nowadays have a more equal share of them."

This passage is interesting and instructive, even though the author's reasoning may not be entirely logical, for it indicates the trend of Teutonic thought with regard to our Colonial Empire. The execution of the Duc d'Enghien in March 1804 had roused the governments of Europe against Napoleon, but only the Tsar Alexander had broken off diplomatic relations in consequence. The French Emperor still awaited on the shore of the English Channel the favourable moment for the invasion of England. His plans, however, suffered a severe blow in the death of Latouche Tréville, his most competent admiral, who was succeeded by Villeneuve, an able commander, but timid and lacking in enthusiasm.

In April 1805 Villeneuve sailed for the West Indies, drawing Nelson and the English fleet after him, and returning in the ensuing month to European waters, whither he was followed by the ships of England. In the meantime the newly made Emperor had been crowned King of Italy at Milan; and he had concluded negotiations with Prussia, under the terms of which the Prussian troops in Hanover were relieved by the French army. Pitt's opportunity for the formation of a third coalition had now arrived. Austria, alarmed by the augmentation of the French army in Italy on the occasion of Napoleon's coronation at the capital of Lombardy, was strengthening her forces and negotiating with Russia for co-operation in the coming war. The Peace of Luneville had left Austria crippled, with her power and prestige in the councils of Europe greatly diminished. But Napoleon's preparations for the invasion of England, leading him to concentrate his attention on that enterprise, appeared to afford her an opportunity of recovering her lost provinces. Already, in October, a sanitary cordon was established on the Austrian frontiers of Italy and Switzerland, nominally for the exclusion of yellow fever, which had broken out in Spain, but in reality to cover ulterior designs. And when the French troops assembled for Napoleon's coronation at Milan, in May 1805, Austria increased her forces in Carinthia and the Venetian provinces.

Pitt, meanwhile, was engaged in forming a third coalition with Russia, Austria, Sweden and Naples against France. Austria was weak in military strength, owing to the reorganisation that was in progress in her army, and it was agreed that Russia should put two armies into the field. Sweden was of little account, and in September Naples came to terms with the French Emperor.

But Napoleon was fully aware of what was going on, and had already turned his eyes towards the Rhine and Danube. His correspondence with his foreign minister, Talleyrand, shows that he contemplated the possibility of a land campaign. Early in August 1805 the idea gained strength, and on the 23rd he wrote to Talleyrand from Boulogne that his squadron had left Ferrol, and if it joined the Brest squadron, and entered the Channel, he would yet be master of England. Failing in the plan of invasion, he would, he said, strike his camp, and march to Germany with 200,000 men. He would not lay down his arms until he had Naples and Venice, and had so enlarged the territories of the Elector of Bavaria that he would have nothing more to fear from Austria.

Villeneuve's orders were to assemble the French and Spanish fleets and set sail from Ferrol. He was to sweep the Channel, raise the blockade of Brest, and so clear the passage for Napoleon's army of invasion. But Villeneuve was wanting in energy and enterprise; on the report that an English fleet was approaching, he returned to safe harbourage at Cadiz, and before the end of the month Napoleon's Grand Army was on the march to the Rhine.

Napoleon's Coronation

The lessons of this period are mainly those of the influence of sea power, and the necessity of preparation for war in time of peace. We see that, without command of the sea, Napoleon could accomplish nothing towards the invasion of England. We also perceive that, failing the maintenance of that command, England would have been a helpless prey in the absence of sufficient strength of land forces. But if command of the sea conferred immunity from invasion, it proved in no way decisive. England, having no army to speak of, could do but little injury to a Continental nation; Trafalgar did not eclipse Austerlitz. Great issues are fought out on land, and Napoleon was finally conquered at Leipzig and Waterloo. What would have happened had the English fleet been destroyed? It is placing the issue on one chance to have no second line of defence in case of defeat at sea. It is like fighting a battle with all your troops in the first line, and no reserve.

Napoleon himself said:

> A nation is very foolish when she has no land forces to rely upon in the event of a picked and warlike army of 100,000 men arriving in her midst.

It has been said and thought by the ignorant that a half-trained force or the uprising of the people would suffice to deal with invasion. But what could such effect against an army of trained and disciplined warriors? What has it ever effected—as recorded in the history of the world?

From the beginning of the formation of national entities until the present time the idea of popular uprisings to repulse foreign invaders has ever been a universal conceit, an indelible vanity that neither the erosion of ages has erased, nor the deluge of blood issuing from them has washed away. Yet, while there exists not an age that has not resounded with the triumphant hoofbeats of invading armies, the truth is there is not a single instance in the whole military history of the world where the mobile armies of a warlike race have been destroyed or defeated by the popular uprisings of a militantly decadent state. [2]

Preparation does not imply merely the provision of armed forces and armament, " neither is money the sinews of war, if the sinews of men's arms in base and effeminate people are failing." [3] Preparation includes the cultivation of patriotic feeling, the direction of the thoughts of the people into unselfish and pure channels, where they will place ideas of nationality and the love of country before the meaner instincts of personal comfort. For man is the primary instrument in war, and no number of guns, armaments or "dreadnoughts" can supply the want of the national and patriotic spirit of self-sacrifice.

All history tells the same tale. Ancient Rome and Sparta were free and strong for many ages, thanks to their armies drawn from the people, but they declined when they put their trust in mercenary troops. Gibbon tells us;" The theory of war was not more familiar to the camp of Caesar and Trajan than to those of Justinian and Maurice. The iron of Tuscany or Pontus still received the keenest temper from the skill of the Byzantine workmen. In the construction and use of ships, engines and fortifications the barbarians admired the superior ingenuity of a people whom they so often vanquished in the field. The science of tactics, the orders, the evolutions, the stratagems of antiquity, was transcribed and studied in the books of the Greeks and Romans.

But the solitude or degeneracy of the provinces could no longer supply a race of men to handle those weapons, to guard those walls, to navigate those ships and to reduce the theory of war to bold and successful practice." It was the patriotism of the French people, their military spirit and love of glory, that enabled them under Napoleon to conquer half Europe, and to carry their arms in triumph from Madrid to Moscow, It was the steady patriotism of the English, in spite of the presence in their midst of unpatriotic factions, that gave them the mastery of the sea, led them for twenty years to contend with the tyranny of Napoleon, and built up their great Colonial Empire.

---

2. *The Valour of Ignorance*. Homer Lea. (see text p.14)
3. Francis Bacon.
4. *Decline and Fall of the Roman Empire*.

Chapter 2

Character of the Opposing Forces

Napoleon had available something over 200,000 men. with 300 guns, organised as follows into the Grand Army.

		The Emperor		
		Chief of Staff, Berthier		
The Guard		Bessieres		6000
		Infantry Divisions	Cavalry Divisions	
1st Corps	Bernadotte	Drouet	Kellerman	
		Rivaud		18,000
2nd Corps	Marmont	Boudet	Lacoste	
		Grouchy		
		Dumonceau		21,000
3rd Corps	Davout	Bisson	Vilannes	
		Friant		
		Gudin		27,000
4th Corps	Soult	St Hilaire	Margaron	
		Vandamme		
		Legrand		
		Suchet		41,000
5th Corps	Lannes	Oudinot	Trielhard	
		Gazan		18,000
6th Corps	Ney	Dupont	Tilly	
		Loison		
		Malher		24,000
		Cuirassiers	Dragoons	

Cav. Reserve Murat	Nansuoty	Klein
	d'Hautpool	Walther
		Beaumont
		Bouvrier
	Dismounted Dragoons	
	Baraguey d'Hilliers	22,000

The Seventh Corps, under Augereau, 14,000 men, was in process of formation. The Bavarians (20,000), Wurtemburgers and Baden Contingent numbered together 28,000, making a total of 219,000 men. Bernadotte was in Hanover; Marmont's Corps round Utrecht, in Holland. He had in addition 50,000 men and 100 guns in Italy under Massena's command, while there was also a force of 20,000 under St Cyr at Naples, which was able to join Massena on conclusion of a treaty of neutrality in September.

Napoleon himself characterised the Grand Army as "the finest army that has ever existed." It is probable that this estimate was justified. We search in vain in the pages of history for the record of an army so well organised, trained and commanded, and inspired by a spirit so warlike and patriotic. It had been in camp undergoing continuous training for eighteen months, and had attained a high standard of efficiency in every respect, whilst it had the great advantage of being trained by those who would lead it in war. While the ranks were filled with young men, there was a valuable leaven of veterans who had fought on the battlefields of Italy and Egypt.

The infantry was composed of infantry of the line and light infantry, formed into demi-brigades (regiments) of two, or in some cases three, battalions, one battalion being allocated to recruiting and reserve purposes. Four demi-brigades formed a division. In action the light troops advanced skirmishing in extended order and taking advantage of all cover; behind them followed the infantry in formed bodies in two or three lines, the attack being made generally in column. In these manoeuvres, in deployments, and in skirmishing and attack in column with the bayonet, the troops had acquired great proficiency. The infantry was armed with a flint gun, effective from one hundred to two hundred yards, but ranging double that distance. Each man carried fifty rounds, and thirty more were in reserve. The cavalry consisted of heavy and light horse—*cuirassiers*, dragoons, hussars and mounted *chasseurs*. They were armed with sabre and pistol, and in some cases with carbines. We know that Napoleon recognised the necessity of equipping cavalry with carbines; on one occasion he wrote:

> How is it possible to carry on any but a defensive war, covered by entrenchments and natural obstacles, if one has not cavalry fairly equal to that of the enemy? An army superior in cavalry will have the advantage of being able to conceal its movements, of having good information of the enemy's movements, and of delivering battle when it pleases. Defeats will have few evil results, and victories will be decisive.

He wrote again. Count Yorck tells us:

> It is universally conceded that the *cuirassiers* have difficulty in using their carbines; but on the other hand it seems absurd that 8000 or 4000 brave men should be exposed to surprise in their cantonments or stoppage on their marches by a couple of light companies. I cannot reconcile myself to seeing 3000 men, picked troops, liable to be overwhelmed by any partisan leader during a popular rising or in a surprise by light troops, or to be arrested on their march by a few good sharpshooters behind a stream or a house; it seems absurd. It is my wish that every man should have a musket, even if it be only a very short carbine. Place some proposal before me so that these 3000 men may not have to depend on infantry to protect them in cantonments, and that they may be able to clear their way if any infantry, inferior in numbers, attack them. As to lancers, see whether we can arm them with both carbine and lance; and if this is impossible, at least one-third of each troop ought to be armed with carbines.

A knowledge of such records of history might save us from having to learn these lessons again from bitter experience. The cavalry regiment was organised in four squadrons. Cavalry brigades were variable in strength. The dragoons were principally employed in reconnoitring and on outpost duties. Like all great commanders, Napoleon knew well how to utilise his cavalry. In action the bulk was assembled in reserve.

The artillery, consisting of guns which had the disadvantage of being of numerous calibres, was formed into divisions, and was generally massed, its fire being concentrated on points of attack. It is noteworthy that co-operation between the three arms had been taught, and was thoroughly understood; the artillery especially had learned to give close support to the infantry. The gunners were armed with musket and bayonet. Troops were well clothed and shod and especial attention was paid to the commissariat. While in general the army lived on the country, magazines were formed when convenient. Each man carried three or four days' supplies, and double that amount was on regimental wagons. The transport was furnished by the contractors of a private company.

In morale the French soldiers were now unequalled. The inauguration of the Empire had added to the power and prestige of Napoleon, whose troops were inspired by his presence, his reviews and his personal distribution of honours at the camp at Boulogne. They possessed that which is half the battle—confidence in themselves and their commanders, and in the certainty of victory. They endured fatigue and privation with remarkable constancy. They were active and enterprising, wonderful marchers, of superior intelligence, and most susceptible to appeals to their love of glory. They knew well how to adapt themselves to the ground and to take advantage of its natural features. Every French soldier had the hope of reward and promotion, for many officers, and even marshals, had risen from the ranks. It could be truly said that each one had a baton in his knapsack.

The regimental officers were excellent, constantly with their men, to whose training and well-being they devoted all their time and interest. General Foy gives us a description of the French advance to the attack:

The action was begun by a cloud of skirmishers, both horse and foot, thrown forward according to a general idea, and not directed as to the detail of their movements. They harassed the enemy; escaped his massed troops by their speed, and his guns by their extended formation. They were relieved with the object of continuing their fire, and they were reinforced to increase their effect. The field artillery came up at a gallop and fired grape and canister at point-blank range. The line of battle broke up in the direction of the attack, the infantry in column, for it had no fire to deliver, the cavalry in regiments or squadrons ready to act in any direction. When the hail of bullets and shot began to thicken, the soldiers advanced at the double, charging with the bayonet, the drums beat the charge, and the air resounded with the oft-repeated cries of 'Forward! Forward!'

This fine army was led by such a galaxy of military talent as the world has never seen. Napoleon himself was at the zenith of his physical and intellectual power.

The assumption of the imperial purple had made him supreme in the state as in the army. He had gained in personal experience of war since he commanded the army of Italy, but he had what was of more value—the experience derived from the study of history, and none of his campaigns excelled in execution the first one, when his previous experience was that of history only.

But he had gained in prestige with the nation and the army, which regarded him as invincible. The great officers of the army, the marshals, were the devoted slaves of him who had raised them to the highest pinnacles of glory. It has been said that "only in despotisms are men in high offices chosen only for their fitness," another factor of success. The decline of military skill in Rome began, Machiavelli [1] tells us, from the time when science and talent were despised, and only those gained distinction who knew how to please the authorities. But in the French army at this period, merit was the sole basis of promotion and reward.

A remarkable feature of the French armies of this epoch is the youth of the officers, a factor that must be taken into account. But the value of youth is nothing new; it is a distinctive feature of all history. At thirty-two, Alexander's career was drawing to a close; at twenty-six, Hannibal was acclaimed leader of the Carthaginian army; at twenty- six, Napoleon Bonaparte was conducting his most brilliant campaign with the army of Italy; at thirty-four Wellington had won the battle of Assaye, and twelve years later, after bringing the arduous Peninsular War to a successful conclusion, he vanquished the great man whose mighty genius was already declining at the early age of forty-six.

In 1805, of the French officers who commanded the corps of the Grand Army, only two, Augereau and Bernadotte, were over forty years of age. Napoleon himself, Lannes, Soult and Ney were thirty-six; Davout was thirty-five and Marmont thirty-one. Half the divisional commanders were between thirty and forty, while only a single one was fifty.

The campaign of Jena, in the ensuing year, when the Prussian army was led to destruction by venerable creatures of routine, furnishes us with another example in this connection. The Duke of Brunswick, "a spendthrift, a loose liver, and a martinet," was seventy; Mollendorf was over eighty; Karlkreuth was sixty-six; even the fiery Blucher was over sixty, and only a few of the younger officers understood Napoleon's revolutionary tactics and strategy. To look to more recent times, most of the successful commanders of the American Civil War were comparatively young men.

When they advance in years, most men lose in energy of both body and mind; they become too old to learn, and too confirmed in their opinions to adopt methods that are new, but that may be rendered necessary by altered conditions. They have a tendency to become soft and enervated, and disinclined to physical discomfort. Their peculiarities become accentuated; their fads are fully developed, and their ideas do not advance with the times. Age may have its advantages, bringing a calm calculation frequently absent in youth and securing its possessor against hasty, impetuous and perhaps ill-advised action. But on the other hand, where an original or novel mode of operations is called for, or where brilliancy and dash are required, younger commanders are more likely to succeed than those who are wedded to antiquated and obsolete ideas. The youth of his generals was not the least factor in Napoleon's success in war. The Emperor himself said that no general had any enterprise left after his forty-fifth year. He proved this in his own person, for in 1815 his genius and his physical powers were already in a profound decline, notwithstanding the brilliant conception of the Waterloo campaign. At Austerlitz he said:

> One has but a short time for war. I am good for another six years, and then I shall have to stop.

And what manner of men were Napoleon's generals? As leaders of men they were unequalled by any in Europe. Accustomed to look to their chief for guidance in all things, they developed little power of initiative on wide theatres of war, though fine tacticians. Bernadotte was clever, and a good leader under the eye of the Emperor, but, like many of the others, incapable of exercising independent command.

The same remarks apply to Marmont, an officer of artillery. Davout was one of the most capable of the marshals, having a wide outlook on the art of war, while his corps was under perfect discipline. Soult had great talents, which he displayed later as an independent commander in Spain. Lannes had no wide intellectual capacity, but possessed those qualities which inspire troops on the field of battle. Ney, "the bravest of the brave," was unequalled as a leader of men in action, but had not the capacity of a great commander. Murat was a splendid leader of cavalry, possessing unexampled courage, activity and dash—but he was no general. Berthier was a model chief of the staff, with a capacity for infinite labour, but he did not learn the great principles of the art of war in twenty campaigns.

Napoleon's system of working is thus described by Jomini:

> The Emperor himself was in reality his own chief of the staff;

holding in his hand a pair of compasses opened by scale to a distance of seven or eight leagues in a straight line (which, reckoning the turnings of the roads, covers a march of nine or ten leagues), bent, nay, often lying, over his map, on which the positions of his army corps and the supposed positions of the enemy were marked by pins of different colours, he arranged his own movements with a certainty of which we can scarcely form a just idea. Moving his compasses rapidly over the map, he calculated in a moment the number of marches for each of his corps to reach any point he wished it to reach on a fixed day, and then, sticking his pins into these new positions, and calculating the rate at which each column would move, he dictated those orders which if they stood alone would entitle him to glory.

It is notable that he rose and dictated his orders at midnight or early dawn. By this method the troops were not kept waiting for orders at night, but received them before the march; while at the same time the latest information, which might have involved a change in orders issued earlier, was thus available.

From the particulars that have been given, some idea may be gained as to this great army, its composition and the methods which led to its wonderful success in war. It has already been mentioned that the Austrian army was still undergoing reform when the war broke out in 1805. The Austrians had learnt something from their defeats on the battlefields of Italy, and many improvements had been introduced into their military methods. New conditions of service were established in 1802, under which men were liable for service between the ages of seventeen and forty; but the system had not attained its full development at the time of the Austerlitz campaign, when, in fact, the Austrian military organisation was in an incomplete state, and they were weak in consequence. Its full effects were not seen until 1809, when corps and batteries were formed on the French model. In imitation of the French, some light battalions were raised; but in 1805 the organisation of the army was still wooden and antiquated, and the movements of troops ponderous and complicated. The method of discipline, though considerably ameliorated; by the efforts of the Archduke Charles, was still harsh, and not calculated to inspire the soldier with patriotic enthusiasm.

The Austrian army in Italy was under the command of the Archduke Charles, one of the ablest generals of his time, but, as will be seen, this army took no part in the Austerlitz campaign. The total strength of the allied forces has been given as:

Main army in Italy	120,000
Army of the Danube	84,000
Tyrol Army	30,000
Reserve	30,000
Russians	140,000
Swedes etc.	26,000
	430,000

It is probable that these numbers are in some cases overestimated. The Austrian armies were organised as follows:—

Army of the Danube

The Archduke Ferdinand

Quartermaster General Field Marshal Mack

Kienmayer	4 brigades	18,000 men
Wernecke	3 divisions	20,000 "
Schwartzenberg	2 divisions	15,000 "
Reisch	3 divisions	13,000 "

Army of the Tyrol

The Archduke John Four divisions 50,000 (including Jellachich)

Army of Italy

The Archduke Charles

Chief of the Staffs Field-Marshal Zach

Four corps

Although nominally under the Archduke Ferdinand, the army of the Danube was in reality commanded by Mack as chief of the staff of the Emperor Francis of Austria. The Austrians had the disadvantage of being directed by a ponderous and stupid Aulic Council. There were two Russian armies, under Kutusoff and Buxhowden, able and enterprising commanders, under whom were Bennigsen, Dokhturoff and Bagration, brave and capable leaders. The Russian soldiers had those characteristics for which they are known today. Nothing could exceed their bravery, their patience and their endurance under all circumstances. The Russian columns were encumbered by enormous trains, an infantry regiment having some fifty wagons and three hundred horses.

Their first army was not expected to reach the Inn before the 20th October; their second army was on the Vistula. There were, in addition to the allied forces detailed, some 20,000 Swedes under Tolstoi on the shores of the Baltic.

The theatre of operations between the Rhine and the Danube was characterised by the densely wooded and mountainous region of the Black Forest, in which the Danube takes its rise; but this country, extending between Basle and Stuttgart, would form a screen to an advancing army, covering its movements, and together with the Jura Mountains, extending on the north and parallel to the Danube, favouring a masked advance towards Nordlingen and Donauworth. With the exception of the Black Forest, then rugged and difficult for the passage of an army, the whole country was rich and fertile, and traversed by good roads; while numerous bridges afforded means of passage across the Danube. Bavaria and Wurtemburg, the territories of Napoleon's allies, extended southward to the borders of the mountainous region of the Tyrol, and as far as the Inn.

The character of Napoleon is the first factor to be noted in considering the causes of success. As he said: "In war, the man is everything." Unity of command, and the concentration of all power in his hands, gave him a great superiority over an enemy who suffered from the disadvantages of divided counsels. The generals of the Allies, although some of them capable commanders, had neither the experience nor prestige of the French leaders; some of them had, indeed, lost prestige in previous campaigns.

Mack had been captured at Civita-Castellana in 1799, and had been a prisoner in Paris; the Archduke Charles had been driven out of Italy by Napoleon in 1797; his chief of the staff was Zach, who had acted in the same capacity at Marengo in 1800; the Archduke John had been vanquished at Hohenlinden in 1800. We meet also with the names of Lusignan, Argenteau, Weyrother and Wukassovich, the latter a brave and able leader, who had all waged unsuccessful war against Napoleon in Italy in 1796. It will be observed throughout this campaign that divided command and consequent dissension among the Allies was a fruitful cause of defeat. Napoleon says on this point:

Nothing is so important in war as an undivided command. For this reason, when war is carried on against a single power, there should be only one army, acting upon one base, and conducted by one chief.

Chapter 3

Advance to the Rhine

On the 23rd August 1805 Napoleon wrote to his Foreign Minister, Talleyrand:
I shall strike my camp here, and order my third battalions to replace my field battalions; on the 23rd September, I shall be in Germany with 200,000 men and in the Kingdom of Naples with 25,000. I shall march on Vienna.

At this time his troops were disposed as follows:—
Bernadotte in Hanover; Marmont at Utrecht; Davout at Ambleteuse; Soult and the Cavalry Reserve, under Murat, at Boulogne; Mortier at Etaples; Ney at Vimereux; Augereau at Brest. Massena commanded the troops in Italy.

Napoleon's plan was to march to the Rhine, and then to the Danube with the Grand Army of 200,000 men, and to defeat the enemy in detail before they could concentrate their forces. Massena was to assemble his forces on the Adige, in Northern Italy and hold the Austrians there; and Saint Cyr was to prepare for the occupation of Naples. Thus the French Emperor would have one strong corps as a holding force in Italy, and seven corps for the invasion of Germany.

The plan of the Allies was for 60,000 Austrians and two Russian armies, amounting to 90,000 men, to operate in the valley of the Danube, under command of the Austrian Emperor, with Field-Marshal Mack as chief of the staff. The Tyrol was to be garrisoned with 50,000 men under the Archduke John, who could reinforce Mack or the Archduke Charles as necessity

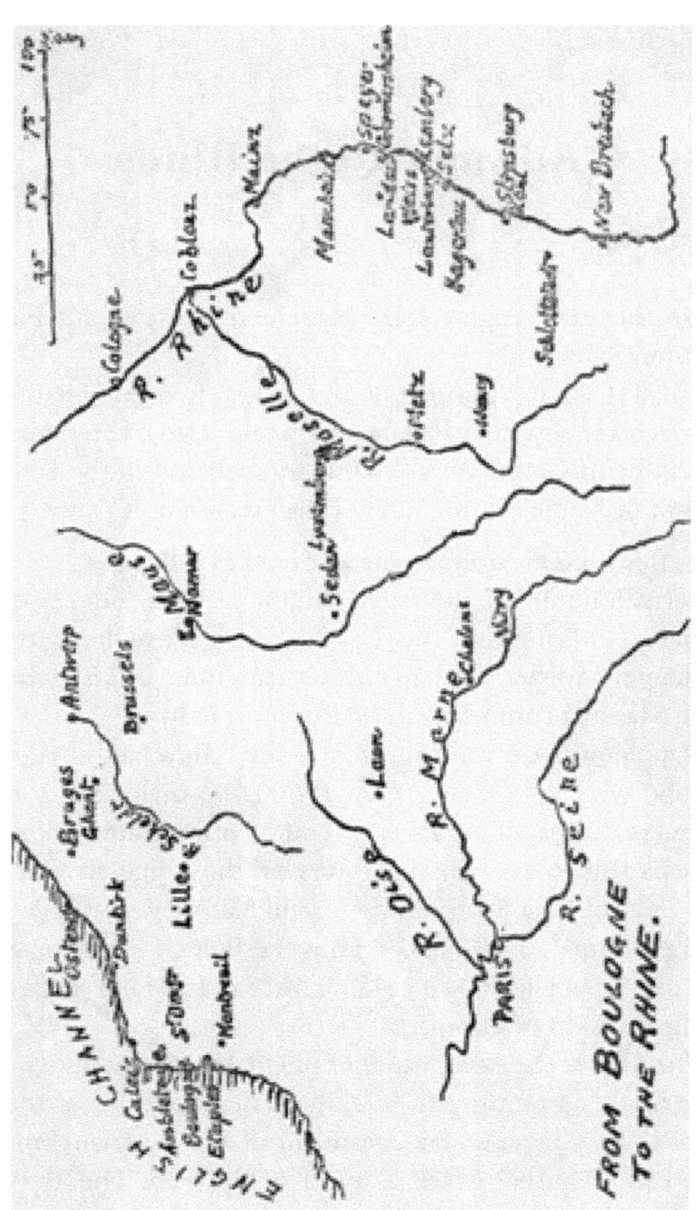

arose, while the Archduke Charles was to take the offensive with 120,000 men in Italy, where it was expected Napoleon would make his main attack. The Allies were also to make a diversion in Naples. The Austrian army, nominally under Ferdinand, but in reality commanded by Mack, was already assembling in the Danube Valley; the Russians were to take the field with two armies. One, of 55,000 men, was to start from Brody on the 20th August, and march to Braunau. on the Inn, to reinforce Mack; the second, of 40,000 men, was to occupy Bohemia, but was still on the Vistula.

But the Austrian plans were drawn up on the assumption that a French army could not reach the Danube before 10th November, and it is related that they made the curious mistake of omitting to allow for the twelve days' difference between the old calendar, observed by Russia, and the new one. In the meantime Mack was to coerce the Bavarians.

Napoleon, having decided to march into Germany, lost no time in preparing for the campaign and carrying out his plans. The army was long since ready. His care in reconnoitring the country through which his armies were to march is instructive. From Boulogne, 25th August 1805, instructions were given to Bertrand to go to Bavaria, making notes of all he saw. From Munich he was to go to Passau and up the Inn to Kufstein.

> He will make a regular reconnaissance, giving the situation of places, their distances, the nature of the roads, the width of the river, the amount of water, the alternate domination of one or other bank, the brooks, the bridges, the fords. He will be accompanied by some Bavarian engineers, but he will be careful to look for himself, and will write what the engineers tell him about the conditions of the river, and what has happened on it.

With similar reports he was to go to Salzburg and back to Munich *via* Wasserburg, thence to Fussen, down the Lech, and to Ingoldstadt and Donauworth, paying heed to the Danube; thence down the Regnitz to the Main, to Bamberg, back to

Ulm, Stuttgart, and thence to Rastadt, "reporting the condition of the roads from a military and general staff standpoint."

Then follows a note of items to be examined and reported on, such as this:

> He will make a detailed reconnaissance of the little river Ilz (which empties into the Danube at Passau), and the nature of the roads and the ground from the source of the Ilz, which comes from the mountains of Bohemia, to the mouth of the Ilz; what is the width of the valley, what is the nature of the roads, the principal towns, and the facilities and the difficulties that an army would have which should cross to the left bank of the Danube, and by these means should turn the Inn and march on Freistadt with the purpose of moving into Moravia."[1]

Other officers were sent with similar instructions. Thus Savary was told "to reconnoitre the roads which, starting from Philipsburg, Bruchsal and Dorlach, crossed the Necker at Heilbronn, Cannstadt and Esslingen, and led thence to the Danube, Dilingen, Gundelfingen and Ulm, as well as the cross-roads between them." Emissaries were despatched to negotiate with Berlin, Bavaria, Wurtemburg and Baden. The newspapers were forbidden to refer to the movements of the French army. Communication was suspended along the left bank of the Rhine; post offices were occupied. In fact, every precaution was taken that might tend to ensure success.

Roads in France were repaired and maps of the theatre of war got ready. Reserve corps of conscripts and the National Guard were formed at Mainz and Strassburg.

The Allies were not so forward in their preparations. They may still have clung to the hope of peace, and at any rate, as has been stated, they did not foresee the possibility of the French army reaching the Danube before November. The Austrian army was not ready, but England would supply money, and Russia would furnish men. The Austrian troops were mobilised in

---
1. *Life of Napoleon*. By Colonel Theodore Dodge, U.S.A. (Gay & Bird).

July, but it was not until the 3rd September that the Emperor Francis declared war. The army under Mack crossed the Inn on the 8th September and reached the Iller before the end of the month. The Bavarians retreated before the Austrian advance, and Mack posted Kienmayer across the Danube at Neuberg and Ingoldstadt to observe them, while he halted with his right on Ulm and his left on Memmingen. The Russian forces, which were on the frontiers of Galicia, were to march to the Inn. But while their enemies were taking counsel the Grand Army was marching.

On the 25th August Napoleon issued orders for the march of the Grand Army to the Rhine. The third battalions of demi-brigades were left at Boulogne, and formed into an army corps for the protection of the coast and the flotilla from English raids. Their grenadier companies had been taken to form Oudinot's division. The 1st Corps was to leave Hanover on the 2nd September and reach Wurzburgon on the 27th. There Bernadotte would be joined by the Bavarians, whom Mack's advance had forced back on Bamberg. The 6th Corps, forming the right wing, left camp on 27th August, and marched by Laon and Vitry upon Schlettstadt; the 5th Corps and the Cavalry Reserve marched by Sedan, Metz and Nancy to Strassburg; Soult with the 4th Corps followed the same route as far as Metz, when he deflected his march to Speyer; Davout marched from Ambleteuse with the 3rd Corps through Lille, Namur and Luxembourg to Mannheim. The 2nd Corps, under Marmont, forming the left wing, marched from Utrecht to Mainz; and Augereau brought the 7th Corps from Bayonne to the neighbourhood of Basle. Napoleon had himself calculated the march of the various corps of his army, and had written from Boulogne on the 31st August:

> The Grand Army is in full march; on 23rd September it will have reached the Rhine.

The distance from Boulogne to Strassburg, 300 miles, was covered in twenty-nine days; and on the 27th September the whole army was across the Rhine. Napoleon remained in Paris until 24th September; he reached Strassburg on the 27th, and from there, three days later, issued a proclamation to the Grand Army:

> Soldiers, the War of the Third Coalition has begun. The Austrian army has crossed the Inn, violated treaties, attacked and driven our ally from his capital. You yourselves have had to hasten by forced marches for the protection of our frontiers; but you have already passed the Rhine. I will not halt until I have ensured the independence of Germany, supported our allies, and lowered the pride of lawless aggressors. We will make no peace without this guarantee. Our generosity shall no longer deceive our policy. Soldiers, your Emperor is in your midst. You are only the vanguard of a mighty people. If necessary that people will rise at my call to destroy this new league, formed by the hatred and the gold of England. But, soldiers, we have forced marches to make, fatigues and privations to endure. We will vanquish all obstacles, and we will not rest until we have planted our eagles upon the territory of our foes.

Napoleon had timely information of the movements of Mack's army. On 10th September Murat reported 60,000 Austrians at Wels, 15,000 at Constance, and 10,000 at Braunau, where a large camp was marked out, and stores had been collected; 80,000 Russians were on the borders of Galicia. His orders for the crossing of the Rhine and the further march of his troops were issued from Paris on the 17th September. This order is summarised as follows:—

> The Cavalry Reserve to cross first, at Mannheim; Nansouty to reach Heidelberg with his *cuirassiers* on the 25th. Klein's dragoons were to advance to Bretten when Soult's first division had passed the river. Bourcier's dragoons were to cross the same day at Kehl, cover Ney's passage, and proceed next day towards Durlach. Beaumont and Hautpoul with their cavalry were to cross at the same place and day, and go to Offenburg and Oberkirch respectively. Other cavalry was to advance on Freiburg, and reconnoi-

tre towards Donauschingen.

The divisions were to follow this cavalry screen in the following order:—

Davout, headquarters Mannheim, to cross there on 26th and push his cavalry on to Sinsheim.
Soult, to cross at Germersheim on 25th, and establish headquarters next day at Bruchsheim.
Ney, to cross at Selz on 25th, and establish head-quarters at Rastadt next day.
Lannes, to cross at Kehl on 25th.
For the further advance to the Danube:
Lannes was to march on 29th, by way of Oberkirch and Rothenburg, to Ulm, 9th October.
Ney, to march, 27th, by Durlach, Stuttgart, Esslngen to Ulm, 7th October.
Soult, by Bruchsal, Ludwigsburg, Gmund to Aalen, 9th October.
Davout, to march by Heidelberg and Heilbronn to Nordlingen, 10th October.
Bernadotte and Marmont, leaving Wurzburg, 1st October, to reach Weissenburg, 9th October.
The Guard, Reserve cavalry, and Artillery park to concentrate at Gmund, 9th October.

The French Emperor had made provision for reserve camps at Mainz and Strassburg, which, together with Breisach and Huningen, were fortified to guard his line of communications.

Mack had reached Wels on the 2nd September, and then moved into Bavaria, hoping to coerce the Bavarians to an alliance or disarmament before the arrival of the French. But his movements were dilatory, and although he entered Munich on the 10th, and pushed his advanced troops down the Iller to Ulm, he failed in his object; the Bavarians withdrew to Bamberg and effected a junction with Bernadotte. Mack then marched up the Danube, and eventually took up an advanced and isolated position on the Iller, with his headquarters at Ulm. The Russians were still far distant. They were not to reach the Inn before the 16th October.

It was not until the 28th September, by which time he realised that Mack had taken up an apparently permanent position on the Iller, that Napoleon issued his final orders for turning them, and cutting them off from the advancing Russians. The following note, written about 22nd September, embodies his first ideas:—

	28th Sept	6th Oct	9th Oct	10th Oct
Bernadotte	Wurzburg	Anspach	Nurnberg	Ratisbon
Marmont	Wurzburg	Anspach	Nurnberg	Ratisbon
Davout	Mannheim	Mergenheim	Anspach	Dietfurt
Ney	Selz	Crailsheim	Weissenburg	Ingoldstadt
Lannes	Strassburg	Gmund	Nordlingen	Neuberg
Soult	Landau	Aalen	Donauworth	

This note is of great interest as showing the clear and methodical way in which the Emperor worked. One of the greatest lessons of this period, as already indicated in the first chapter, is the necessity of preparations for war. For this purpose policy and strategy should go hand in hand; political measures should not be allowed to outstrip the military means necessary for carrying them into effect. Austria should not have joined the coalition until her army was ready. The opening of the campaign affords one of many instances of the outbreak of hostilities without declaration of war. For Napoleon's march to the Rhine may be taken as a hostile act; and war was not declared until his troops were well on their way.

Napoleon's plan was simple in design. Its advantages are obvious, and it appears strange that the Allies should have thought that he would make his attack in Italy. His army was favourably situated for an advance into Germany, the decisive point. Success there would automatically clear the situation in Italy as well. It may be recollected that in 1800, prior to the campaign of Marengo, [2] he conceived a similar plan, but that circumstances

---

2. *Napoleon's Campaigns in Italy.*" By Lt.-Colonel R. G. Burton (Campaign Series, No. 15.)

induced him to alter it and cross the Alps instead of crossing the Danube.

In the present instance Napoleon's plan was correct from every point of view, if only that it was in accordance with the principle of not doing what the enemy wished and expected him to do. He would have the advantage of being in French or allied territory as far as the Austrian frontier on the Inn. He would strike straight at the hostile capital of Vienna, and would be able to place superior forces in the field at the decisive point and moment.

The Austrian plan was faulty from the beginning. In the first place it involved a division of forces and a neglect of the principle of concentration. Political considerations for the protection of their Venetian provinces, as well as the expectation of the French main attack being made in Italy, induced them to take measures to meet a situation that did not arise. They should have been content to leave a holding force in Italy; to abandon, if necessary, the Venetian provinces, in order to concentrate at the decisive point and moment, when the development of the situation should indicate these factors. A successful battle would then have settled everything in their favour. But they had not learnt, even from the bitter experience of the campaigns in Italy in 1796, the fatal effect of a division of force against an active and mobile enemy.

Although having, even without the Russians, a strength equal to the French, they scattered their forces and were weak at all points. In war, as in all things, concentration of effort is the secret of success. Their plans were based on false assumptions as to what the enemy would do, which of itself was sufficient to induce him to do something quite different. When once he had decided to march to Germany and abandon the idea of invading England, Napoleon's plans were made with remarkable certainty, secrecy and celerity. His systematic arrangements for collecting information are worthy of note in view of the principle that timely information regarding the enemy's dispositions and the topographical features of the theatre of operations is an essential

Departure of the Troops

factor of success in war.

His strategical concentration on the Rhine is a model for all time. It will be observed how the different corps were despatched by different roads at a distance from one another so that they would not clash upon the march, and that there would be no difficulty in billeting and supplying them. And they were directed so that the concentration on the Rhine was on a front sufficiently distant from the enemy, but sufficiently limited in extent to satisfy all possible requirements, even should the situation undergo a change. Napoleon's measures to ensure secrecy are well worthy of note and imitation.

In commenting on this initial advance. Count Yorck von Wartenburg says:

> Here we must point out the difference which is shown between Napoleon's strategy and that in vogue nowadays. Napoleon, as appeared from his first plan in 1800, and as now may be more particularly noted here, effected the strategical concentration of his army in the first place on the enemy's flank, so that with a simple forward movement for battle he gained the latter's communications; hence the first encounter could not fail to prove an Ulm or a Jena. Nowadays this can no longer be done. Inasmuch as we must endeavour now to employ all the railway lines for our concentration, and as the enemy also has to make use of all his railway lines leading towards the frontier, there will be in the main a frontal concentration on the part of both combatants, and it will no longer be possible to gain such an enormous advantage with respect to space in the first massing of forces as Napoleon gained here by his strategical marches on the enemy's flank; it will only be possible to gain an advantage in point of time.
>
> "In Napoleon's day there was plenty of time during the march of the armies to the field (for then they had to march) to become acquainted with the enemy's formation and to direct one's own concentration to his flank, assuming of course a correct strategical perception of the

situation. The modern rapidity of mobilisation and of the strategical deployment by means of railways have made the latter a task which must be arranged in all its details during peace; it is therefore impossible to alter it according to the disposition of the enemy's flank. Only after the armies have been massed, and operations have begun, can a superiority of strategical calculation be displayed as to placing oneself on the flank or the rear of the enemy; hence the manoeuvres with which Napoleon was in the habit of opening his campaigns will only be possible after the first few encounters. We can no longer begin immediately with a Jena, but we can still, after a Worth or a Spicheren, choose our lines of operation in such a manner that we may force the enemy to a Gravelotte.

That Napoleon struck the enemy's right flank will be seen in the next chapter, but his first concentration did not effect this. That concentration took place on the Rhine; how indeed could the French Emperor arrange to concentrate on the enemy's flank and gain his communications when that enemy did not cross the Inn until the 9th September? In 1800 his first plan had been to advance against Kray's left flank. In 1805 the disposition of his troops, and especially of Bernadotte, favoured the route taken round the north of the Black Forest. Moreover, had he had to traverse that region, and pass the Danube at its source, he would have been obliged to violate Swiss neutrality and would have presented his flank to the enemy on the Tyrol. His first concentration was, therefore, made with a view to the further advance to the Danube and the passage of that river between Ulm and Ratisbon.

The perfection of the arrangements for the march to the Rhine are worthy of note, the troops marching by different routes for convenience of supply and billeting; and, while widely separated during the march, they were concentrated on the Rhine within a space which admitted of a rapid closer concentration when required. Bernadotte, it will be observed, was directed by a route that brought him quickly to the support of the Bavarians. The use of the cavalry to cover the advance is noteworthy, and in accordance with modern principles.

Chapter 4

From the Rhine to Ulm

Napoleon's fresh orders of 28th September provided for turning the enemy by a shorter line.

Davout was to march through Heidelberg and Ingelfingen to Neuberg, 8th October.

Soult, through Heilbronn and Nordlingen to Donauworth, 8th October.

Lannes, by Ludwigsburg and Aalen to Neresheim, 8th October.

Ney, through Stuttgart and Esslingen to Heidenheim, 7th October.

The Cavalry Reserve was to make a demonstration through the passes of the Black Forest, and, marching through Stuttgart and Heidenheim, to reach Donauworth, 8th October.

Bernadotte was to march through Anspach in Prussian territory to Eichstadt by 8th October, and thence manoeuvre towards Ingoldstadt.

Marmont, having crossed the Main at Mainz, to move through Aschaffenberg in the direction of Nassenfels, 8th October.

These movements cut the Austrian line of retreat down the valley of the Danube; and Napoleon wrote to Bernadotte, 22nd September, from Strassburg:

> If only I am lucky and Mack remains three or four days more on the Iller and in the Black Forest, I shall surround his army, and only its shattered remnants will escape.

In pursuance of the orders of 28th September, the French corps occupied on the 2nd October a frontage of some ninety miles between Stuttgart and Wurzburg. The Bavarians joined Bernadotte at the latter place. Mack, deceived by the movements of the cavalry in the Black Forest, thought that the French were advancing from that direction, but his plans were not thought out, which Napoleon quickly perceived, for he wrote to Joseph:

> The enemy is marching and countermarching and appears to be embarrassed.

Mack's forces were still scattered. Jellachich was in the Vorarlberg with 14,000 men; Riesch had 19,000 and Schwarzenberg 12,000 along the Iller and Danube from Kempten to Gunzburg. Kienmayer had been detached with 6000 men in the direction of Ingoldstadt to watch the Bavarians. His troops also were scattered. Reinforcements called up by Mack were advancing from the Tyrol.

Napoleon arrived at Ludwigsburg on the 4th October. The French corps, favoured by fine weather, continued their march, and Mack at length had suspicions that his flank was being turned, for he had information from Kienmayer that strong forces of the enemy were marching on Donauworth.

Mack accordingly moved towards Ulm on the 5th, collecting his army on the line Gunzburg-Illereichen. Kienmayer concentrated at Neuberg, on observing the approach of the strong hostile columns, and Jellachich was ordered to march to Biberach by the 8th October. Napoleon, who was this day at Gmund, perceived that the enemy was concentrating on Ulm. The French advance to Nordlingen had now contracted their front to sixty miles.

Napoleon reached Nordlingen on the 6th. He was expecting a battle at Donauworth, and his front was this day reduced to fifty miles between Heidenheim and Eichstadt. He could now concentrate on his centre in twenty-four hours or on either flank in forty-eight hours. His corps were in position as follows:—

Bernadotte and the Bavarians at Weissenburg.

Marmont at Wassertrudingen.

Davout at Oettingen.

Soult at Nordlingen. His advanced guard captured the bridge at Munster in the evening.

Lannes at Neresheim.

Bessières, with the guard, at Aalen.

Ney near Heidenheim, protecting the communications towards Ulm.

Murat near the Danube.

Baraguey d'Hilliers and Bourcier, with their dragoons, protected the right wing at Geisslingen.

D'Hautpoul's and Nansouty's divisions of *cuirassiers* formed rearguards behind Bessières and Soult respectively. Finding no enemy, Napoleon prepared to cross the Danube. Mack wrote this day to the Aulic Council that the enemy were apparently acting against his communications, but he remained inactive.

The French began to cross the Danube next day, 7th October.

Murat crossed at Donauworth and marched towards Rain.

Soult crossed at the same place, and moved on Augsburg.

Bernadotte was at Eichstadt.

Marmont was at Treuchtlingen. Lannes was at Nordlingen.

Davout was at Monheim.

D'Hautpoul was at Nordlingen.

Nansouty was at Donauworth.

Ney was at Giengen.

Bourcier and Baraguey were in support at Heidenheim. Ney had instructions to approach nearer to the Danube as soon as the army was across. Mack, hearing that the French were crossing, made arrangements to concentrate on Gunzburg, detaching Auffenberg, with eight battalions and thirteen squadrons, to Wertingen, and preparing to follow with a view to attacking the French as they crossed. He appears to have known nothing of their strength. Jellachich was directed to march to Ulm. This day

Napoleon, who was with Soult, wrote that "the enemy has no time to lose in order to avoid entire destruction."

Murat, joined by Lannes and Nansouty, recalled from Rain, defeated and dispersed Auffenberg's column at Wertingen on the 8th October. On this day—

Bernadotte crossed the Danube at Ingoldstadt, Soult approached Augsberg.

Davout crossed at Neuberg, and marched towards Aichach.

Marmont reached Neuberg.

Bessières and D'Hautpoul were at Donauworth.

Ney was on the march, in two columns, towards Ulm *via* Langenau, and towards Gunzburg *via* Ingelfingen.

That night an unsuccessful attempt was made to capture the bridge at Elchingen. Napoleon, who was at Donauworth, was urging his lieutenants to vigorous action. Thus he wrote to Davout: "Lose no time and let me know that you occupy Aichach"; and to Soult: "Send me at least three or four thousand prisoners."

On the Austrian side this day Mack did nothing. Kienmayer marched to Dachau. The weather had hitherto been fine, but on this day heavy rain set in, and continued for a week.

The French front was now contracted to thirty-five miles. Bourcier with his dragoons was at Stuttgart; Ney was on the Brenz, facing Ulm, to cover the right flank and communications of the army and bar the way to Bohemia. Bernadotte completed the passage of the river at Ingoldstadt on the 9th. Napoleon was with Murat and Lannes at Zusmarshausen for the night.

Mack had concentrated near Gunzburg, but he heard of the defeat of his detachment at Wertingen; then Ney came up and took possession of the bridge opposite Gunzburg, and Mack retired to Ulm. Ney occupied Gunzburg with one division. Kienmayer continued his retreat to the Inn.

Napoleon did not expect the Austrians to remain at Ulm, as their magazines were at Memmingen, and their greatest interest was not to break communication with the Tyrol. He expected the Russians to advance to Mack's relief, and on this review of the situation he formed his army into two groups. Murat, under whose orders Ney was placed, and Lannes were to march on Ulm. Bernadotte, with Marmont and the Bavarians, were sent to Munich to oppose the expected Russian advance, but were to continue to hold Ingoldstadt.

Napoleon went to Augsberg on the 10th, where Soult was. There the information reached him that Mack was still in Ulm, and that the Russians were not advancing. Davout was at Dachau; Marmont at Pottmes. Murat reached Burgau. In the light of this information, the French Emperor resolved to march with his whole army to cut off Mack from the Tyrol and hold him in Ulm, leaving only Bernadotte and Davout to oppose any Russian advance.

Soult was accordingly to make for Landsberg.

Marmont to march on Augsberg.

Lannes to follow Murat to Burgau.

Bernadotte and Davout to march on Munich, the former having instructions to clear the enemy out of the country between the Isar and the Lech.

Ney was still at Gunzburg, where he prepared for a general advance on Ulm next day. Dupont, with a division and Bourcier's dragoons, formed the right at Albeck. On the morning of the 11th Napoleon wrote to Murat:

> Tonight I shall order Marshal Lannes to pass to Burgau. I do not yet consider matters finished on your side. The enemy being surrounded will fight. He is being reinforced from the Tyrol and Italy; he can therefore oppose you in a few days with more than 40,000 men. Your reserve with Ney and Lannes Corps, which number in all fifty or sixty thousand men, should therefore march close together, so that they can unite in six hours and crush the enemy. The Russians are approaching rapidly; march on the enemy, then, wherever he may be, but with caution and close together; it he escapes you, he will be stopped on the Lech. Moreover, in a successful battle, with the spirit by which the troops are animated, half the enemy would fall into

your hands.

Mack now conceived the idea of escaping to Bohemia by way of Albeck, Heidenheim and Nordlingen, and at the same time cutting the French communications. To cover this movement he intended to leave the corps of Jellachich on the Iller. This project was a good one, and gave some chance of success if carried out with vigour.

Murat, knowing Napoleon's idea that Mack would attempt to escape to the south, directed Ney to cross with his whole force to the right bank of the Danube. But Ney wisely left Dupont's division and Baraguey d'Hilliers' dragoons on the left bank, with orders to march on Ulm, where it was supposed only a few of the enemy would remain.

Thus on the 11th, Dupont, with his 6000 men, met the enemy's 25,000 under the Archduke Ferdinand at Haslach. He deployed his whole division in one line, and held the Austrians at bay until nightfall, when he was driven back on Albeck, and retreated to Langenau and the Brenz, having lost a third of his force, and his baggage. Baraguey d'Hilliers, who was at Langenau, had been ordered to support him, but no orders reached him. However Dupont had succeeded in convincing Mack that his road was barred, and he hesitated in uncertainty until the 13th, when it was too late to carry out his project. His vacillation is indicated in a letter which the Archduke Ferdinand wrote to the Austrian Emperor on the 12th:

> General Mack has already projected and put into execution today three absolutely different plans.

On the 11th the Emperor remained with the Guard at Augsberg, where Marmont joined him.

Soult reached Landsberg.

Lannes reached Burgau.

Davout reached Dachau.

Kienmayer retired on the Inn, where he heard that 8000 Russians had arrived at Braunau.

Bernadotte entered Munich on the 12th October.

Davout and D'Hautpoul remained at Dachau to watch the Russians.

Soult had been directed on Memmingen to block the enemy's way to the Tyrol.

Marmont entered Tannhausen.

Murat, with Lannes and his cavalry, was on the Rothbach on the line Wissendorn-Pfaffenhausen-Falheim.

Ney, who was on the right bank of the Danube, less Dupont and Bourcier on the left bank, fell back behind the Brenz. Bessières was at Zusmarshausen.

Mack's way to Bohemia had been opened by Ney's movements under Murat's orders, and by the defeat of Dupont. But the Austrian did not take immediate advantage of this chance. He decided to march on the 13th towards Heidenheim, and attack the French communications.

But it was then too late, for he was shut in on every side, and Napoleon could truly say that he had destroyed the enemy merely by marches. In two more marches the circle would be complete. Anticipating success, the Emperor said: "On the 14th, the day of battle, the enemy will be annihilated, for he is hemmed in on every side"; and "Never will so much have been decided in so short a time."

He wrote to Soult: "The decisive moment has arrived." But, true to his principle of collecting all available troops for battle, he also wrote in a letter to Murat on the 12th:

> I intend, should the enemy remain in his present positions, and be prepared to accept battle, to fight, not tomorrow, but the next day, so that Marshal Soult and his 30,000 men may take part in it; he will march to the enemy's right flank, and attack when he has turned it, a manoeuvre which will ensure a decisive result.

His attention to details is shown in this same letter:

> Have a bridge thrown over the Danube as near as possible to your line opposite Albeck, so that the corps in Albeck may be in communication with the rest of the army. Or-

der the generals to inspect the arms and ammunition, and assemble all your men who may have been detached with the baggage train; send away the baggage and wagons beyond Burgau, to park in the fields, so that there shall be nothing on the main roads.

He also gave Murat directions regarding provision for the wounded, doctors, ambulances and supplies. He wrote to Otto the same day:

> The discouragement of the Austrian army is unexampled. Our worst regiments of *chasseurs* charge and put to night heavy regiments of *cuirassiers*.

Far different was the spirit of the French. The Fifth Bulletin says:

> The Emperor was on the bridge over the Lech when Marmont's corps defiled. Each regiment was formed in a circle, and he spoke to them of the situation of the enemy, the imminence of a great battle, and his confidence in them. This harangue took place during terrible weather. Heavy snow was falling, the troops were up to their knees in mud, and suffered from the intense cold; but the Emperor's words were of fire. The soldiers forgot their privations and fatigues and were impatient for the hour of combat.

Mack, instead of concentrating for his proposed stroke towards Heidenheim, lingered in Ulm, and detached Jellachich to the Vorarlberg.

On the night of the 12th the French Emperor drove thirty miles to Pfaffenhausen, and at once sent Ney to reinforce Dupont, whom he ordered back to Albeck. The Guard was called into Gunzburg. Napoleon himself joined Ney at Kussendorf.

This day he issued a proclamation to the army:

> Soldiers! It is only a month since you were encamped on the ocean opposite England. Less than a fortnight since, we passed the Rhine, the Wurtemburg Alps, the Neckar, the

Danube and the Lech; these famous barriers of Germany have not delayed our march a day, an hour, an instant. Remember that tomorrow you fight against the allies of the English. Soldiers! tomorrow will be a hundred times more famous than the day of Marengo. I have placed the enemy in the same position. I can say to my people: 'Your emperor and your army have done their duty. Do yours, and 200,000 conscripts whom I have called will rush with forced marches to reinforce our second line.'

Mack left Ulm on the 13th, marched along the left bank of the Danube, and sent 25,000 men under Wernecke towards Heidenheim, while another column under Loudon was directed down the river towards Gundelfingen. Wernecke's vanguard reached Heidenheim; and the second column drove off a French post at the bridge of Elchingen; but the French destroyed the bridge and stopped the Austrian advance. The latter occupied the heights of the town. Mack, instead of using all his strength on this enterprise, remained in Ulm with the bulk of his forces.

This day the Austrian General Spangen surrendered to Soult at Memmingen with 5000 men. Jellachich retreated into the Vorarlberg, and Soult turned back towards Ulm.

Dupont was sent to Albeck on the 14th October.

At dawn on the same day Ney moved on Elchingen, which was held by 15,000 Austrians, who occupied a strong position among gardens and enclosures. After a stubborn fight, the Austrians were driven back on Ulm with the loss of 3000 prisoners and 20 guns. Ney then established his headquarters at Albeck. Lannes took up a position on the heights of Pfuhl, overlooking Ulm.

Marmont arrived at Kirchberg on the Iller.

Napoleon established his headquarters at the abbey of Elchingen, and sent orders to Lannes and the greater part of the cavalry to come up at daybreak. The idea was to deliver the main attack on the left bank, Marmont holding the enemy in check on the south.

On hearing of Mack's advance on Elchingen, Wernecke had

turned back with a view to attacking Ney in rear, but he was repulsed by Dupont, and retired to Nerenstetten. Mack took up a position on the Lahr-Mohringen heights in front of Ulm, on the left bank of the Danube.

Ulm is dominated on the north by the heights of the Michelsberg and the Tuillerie, which were fortified, but on the morning of the 15th, when the various French corps closed in, the Michelsberg was occupied by Ney and the Tuillerie by a division of Soult's corps. Lannes crossed the river at Elchingen, and prolonged Ney's left.

Mack retired into Ulm, and refused to surrender when summoned. Dupont held off Wernecke, who had been joined by the Archduke Ferdinand from Ulm with 1000 cavalry.

Soult reached Biberach.

On the 16th, after an hour's bombardment, negotiations for surrender were reopened with the Austrians. Murat was despatched with the cavalry and Dupont's and Oudinot's divisions to attack Wernecke.

Mack agreed to surrender on the 25th if not relieved. Wernecke retreated on the 17th but was delayed by his baggage train and was vigorously pursued.

On the 18th Wernecke, with 2500 men, surrendered at October Trochtelfingen. The Archduke Ferdinand rode off with 1000 horse and was pursued by Murat from Albeck to Nurnberg, but made good his escape.

Napoleon succeeded in persuading Mack to surrender without further delay, and on the 20th October the Austrian army in Ulm filed past Napoleon, to the number of 27,000 men, with 80 guns. During the scene of surrender, an Austrian officer wrote in his journal,

> Napoleon in the uniform of a common soldier, with a grey coat singed on the elbows and tails, a slouch hat, without any badge of distinction, on his head, his arms crossed behind his back, and warming himself at a campfire, conversed with vivacity and made himself agreeable.

He was throughout this campaign no longer the Emperor, but the general commanding the army in the field. If Napoleon's masterly movement to the Danube is followed on the map it will be seen that it explains itself. The use of the cavalry is especially noteworthy, as well as the ordered march of the corps, gradually closing in as they drew nearer to the enemy. While Murat covered the right flank of the advancing army in its movement round the Black Forest, the cavalry of each corps covered the advance. The cavalry do not appear to have obtained much information regarding the enemy, whose general situation only seems to have been known to Napoleon until he arrived at Augsberg on the 10th October. Until then the situation was generally enveloped in the fog of war. This want of information led to a greater dispersion of force than would have been necessary had the Emperor known that the Russians were still so far off. But the situation has to be examined as it presented itself at the time, and not in the light of information not then available. The withdrawal of troops from the left bank of the Danube on the 11th left the French communications dangerously exposed, and opened an avenue of escape to Mack. This appears to have been due to Murat misunderstanding the situation, and ordering Ney to cross the Danube. But for the latter taking upon himself to leave Dupont's division on the other side, an entirely fresh situation would have had to be provided for.

Certainly Napoleon appears to have conclusively made up his mind that Mack would attempt to break out to the south, but his letter to Murat on the morning of the 11th shows that he had given that commander every latitude. He has been criticised for having finally succeeded in concentrating round Ulm only 120,000 out of his 200,000 men. But he would surely have been open to censure had he not provided for the possibility of the advance of a hostile force from the Inn, where he knew preparations had been made for a base at Braunau; and from the Tyrol, where the Archduke John had a considerable army.

In its masterly conception, its execution, and its results, the advance to the Danube furnishes one of the most remarkable episodes in the history of war. From beginning to end the influence of the master mind, the great driving force, is evident. Only where his hold on events slackens for a moment is there any occurrence to interfere with the mechanical progress of this great manoeuvre.

The Austrians in the first place took up a position that was too far advanced, and thus laid themselves open to being surrounded. The allied forces were not only unwisely disseminated over the whole theatre of war, but on this theatre of operations also. Mack's active operations, when he undertook any, were partial and half-hearted, undertaken by portions of his force at a time, and thus open to defeat in detail. We see this in his sending Auffenberg to Wertingen, in Jellachich's movement to the Tyrol, and in the attempts north of the Danube on every occasion. The character of the commander is reflected throughout on the course of events.

On the 6th October he was already aware that his communications were being threatened, and he should at once have taken action with his full strength, and made dispositions to attack the enemy as they were crossing the Danube. Instead, he waited until next day and then despatched Auffenberg, unsupported, to Wertingen, with the result that might have been expected. He might still have marched to the Vorarlberg, joined hands with the Archduke John, and have stood with the Prussians on the line of the Inn. Instead of this he despatched Jellachich to the Vorarlberg, and with a portion of his reduced force made an attempt on the French communications.

His chance came when Dupont was driven back on the 11th, and an enterprising commander might then not only have inflicted considerable damage on the enemy, but escaped into Bohemia. On this point Napoleon says:

> When you are occupying a position which the enemy threatens to surround, collect all your force immediately and menace him with an offensive movement.

But Mack's measures were all half-measures: "Half-hearted

measures never attain success in war, and lack of determination is the most fruitful source of defeat." The truth of this aphorism is nowhere more fully exemplified than in this campaign.

Criticism should not be destructive only, and it is interesting to consider what Mack might have done in view of the general situation and with the resources at his disposal. It has already been indicated that the position he took up was too advanced. But the French invasion was expected neither so soon nor in such great force. When the enemy appeared in great force on the Danube, the Russian army advancing to his support was still a fortnight distant. But he might have gained some days by concentrating his forces, and attacking the first of the hostile columns that crossed the river. He could then have fallen back on the Isar as a first line of defence, his left flank resting on the Archduke John in the mountains of the Tyrol.

Having made what stand he could there, he would have fallen back to the Inn, where he had in Braunau a strongly fortified place, and where the front to defend was still narrower. The enemy's advance might have been further delayed by the destruction of the bridges over these rivers. If the Russians came up in time, he could have held the line of the Inn; if forced back before their arrival, on the 20th October, he could have pursued the tactics which we shall see were subsequently employed by Kutusoff in his retreat towards Vienna. A concentration would have been effected, and the allies could have stood for battle in the strong position of St Polten with some hope of success.

But Mack was not the man to undertake any such methodical operations. Weak and vacillating, as his opponent was strong and determined, he frittered away his time and his force in futile and half-hearted measures.

CHAPTER 5

From Ulm to Austerlitz

Although Napoleon's plans had hitherto been crowned with success, there were factors in the general European situation that were not favourable to his views, either with regard to his immediate operations or future designs. It has been related how Bernadotte crossed the neutral Prussian territory of Anspach. This violation of neutrality aroused great indignation in Prussia. It appeared at one time as though the Prussian King would declare war, thus placing a hostile army and territory in Napoleon's rear. But the French Emperor managed to smooth the affair over, and it was to some extent condoned by the passage of Russian troops through Prussian territory, by permission. But the Russian Emperor went in person to Berlin and attempted to draw Frederick William into the coalition. In November the two monarchs entered into a defensive treaty at Potsdam, and in a manner worthy of the modern successor of the Prussian King swore a dramatic oath of eternal friendship over the tomb of Frederick the Great.

The designs of the allies and the possibility of hostile action on the part of Prussia did not, however, in any way deter the French Emperor from carrying out his plans. Indeed, the best thing for him to do in any case was to gain a victory. Retreat would weaken him in both a political and military sense. A victory would reduce the strength of his enemies, and would probably decide the Prussian Government to maintain neutrality. Moreover, he knew that Prussia would take some months to

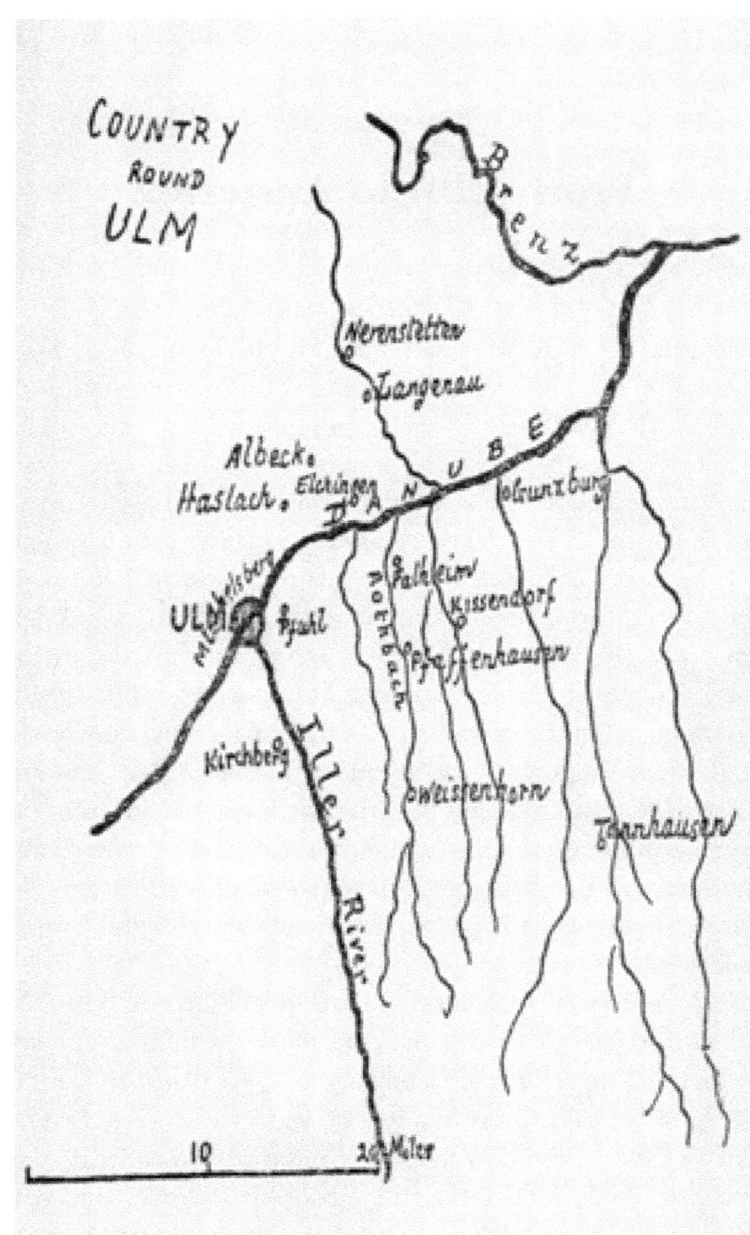

prepare for war.

The second event which disturbed the French Emperor was the news of the battle of Trafalgar, which was to have so great an effect on the destinies of Europe. On 25th September Villeneuve, who commanded the French fleet at Cadiz, received orders to pass through the Straits of Gibraltar and proceed to Naples to co-operate with the army there under St Cyr. He was to engage the enemy wherever found. On 21st October the combined French and Spanish fleets were destroyed off Trafalgar by Nelson's English fleet. Although the destruction of his fleet did not affect the military situation on the Continent, it dimmed to some degree the lustre of Napoleon's arms.

Sloane says that " it produced a depressing effect on the ranks of the Grand Army," but it does not appear on what evidence this statement is based. Great issues are fought out on land, and the effects of Trafalgar were still remote. Napoleon received the news of the destruction of his fleet with calm philosophy; but no doubt he realised its full significance, as he had always realised the value of sea power, which he had hitherto considered the principal and constant aim of his policy.

The events of this period prove that, while dominant sea power is a necessity to the very existence of an insular empire, it is not essential to land campaigns on the part of a Continental nation. It proves that, while Nelson and his storm-beaten ships may have stood between Napoleon and the dominion of the world, they in no way influenced his domination of the Continent. The absence of an effective army rendered England powerless to injure Napoleon in Europe, except by the formation of political leagues and the subsidising with gold of military powers.

Napoleon had already, when he saw that success at Ulm was certain, turned his thoughts to subsequent Napoleon's operations. On the 12th October Berthier wrote to Davout: "On completion of this affair, his Majesty will return and cross the Inn immediately." The further advance of his army was facilitated by the presence of Bernadotte on the Isar, whither he had been despatched, as already related, to hold back the Russians and cover the operations round Ulm.

His general idea now was to pursue and destroy Kutusoff's army before it was joined by the second army under Buxhowden, and to finish the campaign early, in case the Prussians should decide on hostilities. The French Emperor on the 20th October issued orders for the concentration of the army on the Isar. On the 21st October he left Elchingen for Augsberg, where he established his principal magazine. Here a central depot was formed and supplies were collected. Hitherto the rapidity of the march and the necessity for secrecy had not allowed of the formation of magazines. The troops had lived on the country, but such a system, or want of system, while it was detrimental to discipline, would have been disastrous in the event of scarcity or in the event of the army suffering reverses. The valley of the Danube between Ratisbon, where the river takes a turn to the south-east, and Munich, which is approached by the foothills of the Tyrolese Alps, is about a hundred miles in width. But towards the east it gradually narrows until, when the Enns is reached, the mountain spurs descend to within twenty-five miles of the Danube, while in the neighbourhood of Vienna the Weinarwald approaches still nearer to the city and the river.

Thus an army marching down this valley, at first upon a wide front, finds itself more restricted laterally as regards good communications as it descends the stream, for the main roads available for use become fewer in number.

While the left flank of the army is protected by the Danube, the second largest river of Europe, and already at Passau over two hundred and thirty yards in width and sixteen feet deep; at first its right and subsequently its rear is obviously exposed to any advance from the Tyrol and from Italy. From the Vorarlberg roads lead to Munich down the valley of the Iller and the Lech. From the Tyrol also, from Trent and Innsbruck, a good road ran in 1805 down the valley of the Inn to Wassenburg and Muhldorf. From Trieste and Venice there were roads to Salzburg, and that by way of Leoben, down the valley of the Muhr to Vienna, by which Napoleon had advanced after his campaign in Italy in 1797.

Napoleon, then, in advancing from Ulm to Vienna, had to pay special attention, at first to his right flank and then to his rear, in view of the presence of Austrian armies in Italy and the Tyrol.

A feature of the Danube valley is the succession of rivers, the Inn, Traun, Ips, Enns and Traisen, which would afford a succession of rearguard positions for an army retreating on Vienna; and, when the bridges were broken, a series of obstacles to the pursuing force. French The orders now issued provided for the Movements following movements:—

Davout, from Dachau to Freising.

Marmont, from Weissenhorn to Munich.

Bernadotte to concentrate at Munich.

Lannes, with Nansouty's *cuirassiers*, from Nordlingen to Landshut, where Napoleon established his head-quarters on the 24th.

Soult, from Memmingen to Landsberg.

Augereau, from Huningen to Kempten, at the base of the Vorarlberg, where he covered the army from the direction of the Tyrol.

Ney remained at Ulm for the present.

Murat stood at Hohenlinden, with a portion of his cavalry.

Augsberg and Ingoldstadt were held by some cavalry and the divisions of Dupont and Dumonceau, who formed a rearguard, and would march along the Danube towards Passau.

The movements detailed above were completed by the 25th October. Kutusoff, with 40,000 Russians, had on the 20th reached Braunau, on the Austrian frontier, where a depot had been formed. Kienmayer was at Muhldorf, and Merveldt soon joined with reinforcements, making a total of 20,000 men.

The Archduke John was in the Tyrol with 20,000 men; and Ferdinand commanded 10,000 men in Bohemia. The Archduke Charles was holding the Adige. The Austrians wished to hold the line of the Inn, but Kutusoff judged it better to retire, hoping to join the second Russian army, and to give time for the Archduke Charles to co-operate, and for Prussia to act.

On the 23rd October Kutusoff heard from Mack, who passed Braunau on his way to Vienna, of the disastrous events at Ulm, and of the approach of the French. The Russian general at once decided to retreat down the right bank of the Danube to the line of the Enns. Leaving a rearguard on the right bank of the Inn, he destroyed all the bridges across that river and reached Wels on the 27th. Orders to make a stand on the Inn came from Vienna too late.

Napoleon was at Munich with Marmont and the Guard on 26th October.

Soult was *en route* to Muhldorf.

Lannes at Landshut.

Davout at Dorfen.

Bernadotte at Wasserburg.

Ney had left Ulm for Landsberg, where he covered the right flank of the advance.

Bourcier and Baraguey with cavalry at Augsberg and Ingoldstadt.

Dupont and Dumonceau, forming the rearguard, advancing down the Danube on Passau, at the junction of the Inn with that river.

Next day Murat with the cavalry reached Muhldorf, followed by Soult.

Davout arrived at Muhldorf. Lannes advanced towards Braunau.

Bernadotte, with Marmont in reserve, reached Wasserburg and Rosenheim, where the bridges were then repaired. Murat saw to the repair of the bridges over the Inn at New Oetling and Marktl; and crossed next day, when he marched to Burghausen, followed by Davout. Bernadotte crossed the river; Marmont reached Wasserburg; Lannes—Braunau; Soult—Muhldorf; Napoleon was at Haag.

Braunau was occupied without opposition, and the advanced base, hitherto at Augsberg, was established there. Napoleon rode to Muhldorf on the 29th, and arrived at Braunau in the evening, finding it a strong fortress filled with stores and ammunition.

The army was now directed on Wels and Lambach.

Murat, followed by Soult, who crossed the Inn at Muhldorf, and Davout, who reached Burghausen, forming the first line, advanced to Altheim.

Marmont was directed on Steyer, to turn the enemy's left should he make a stand on the Traun; he reached Tittmoning on the 30th.

The same day Bernadotte entered Salzburg. Ney marched on Innsbruck, where he would be in a position to clear the Tyrol, and deal with any advance from that direction on the part of the Archduke John. He was supported by Augereau at Kempten.

The Russians continued their retreat, but Napoleon, who remained some days at Braunau, now advised caution in following them up. He had not met them yet, and did not know their qualities; but he wrote to Murat: "The Russians are not yet broken; they know how to attack."

On the 31st October Murat marched on Lambach. Lannes was at Scharding, moving on Linz.

Soult, at Obernberg, making for Wels.

Davout, at Ried, making for Lambach.

Marmont, at Strasswaldchen, moving on Vocklabruck.

This day a Russian rearguard held the right bank of the Traun at Lambach, and burnt the bridge there, thus covering the retreat of their main body. The weather, which had continued to be wet, now became cold and dry. Napoleon this day, 1st November, reached Ried and halted a day on the Traun. On the 2nd November Lannes was at Linz.

Soult at Wels.

Davout at Lambach.

Murat beyond Wels.

Bernadotte and Marmont were moving towards the Tyrol to gain touch with Ney and cover the right flank of the advancing army.

The Russians were on the Enns at Strenberg; the Austrians

PRINCE MURAT

under Merveldt at Steyer. Next day Kutusoff continued his retreat to Molk, and Merveldt passed through Altenmarkt to the Muhr. Kutusoff stopped at Amstetten, covering the single road from the Molk defiles.

On the 4th November Murat crossed the Enns and advanced on Amstetten, followed next day by Lannes and Soult. At that place he was held back for a time by the Russian rearguard under Bagration.

Marmont and Bernadotte had been directed to regain touch with the main army; they followed Davout, who marched by way of Kremunster to Steyer, which he reached on the 4th, and Marmont on the 5th.

On the 6th November Gazan's and Klein's (Cavalry) divisions were despatched across the Danube at Linz, and next day these and the divisions of Dupont and Dumonceau, which were coming from Passau, were formed into a new corps under Marshal Mortier, who was to march down the left bank of the Danube.

At Linz a flotilla was formed, so that the army might be able to cross at any moment, and, as the Emperor said, "so that the river would no longer exist" for him.

This day Napoleon wrote to Murat complaining that he sent him no information, and telling him to write two or three times a day: "You must have a cavalry picket of six men every three leagues to carry your letters. This will enable you to pass your correspondence very rapidly."

Kutusoff reached St Polten on the 7th November, and from here Merveldt marched up the Enns to threaten the French right, orders having come from Vienna for a stand to be made on the Enns.

As it was expected that the enemy would stand at St Polten, Davout was sent to march to Lilienfeld *via* Gaming; by this manoeuvre he would turn the enemy's left, cover the right flank of the French advance, and relieve congestion on the one road that led to Vienna from Linz. Marmont was ordered to Leoben to cover the right from the Tyrol.

While Napoleon was at Linz a deputation arrived from the

Austrian Emperor, asking for an armistice. But the terms offered by Napoleon, including the abandonment by Austria of Venice and the Tyrol, and the retirement of the Russians to Poland as a preliminary, could not be accepted by Francis. Napoleon had, indeed, nothing to gain by a cessation of hostilities at this stage. Delay would admit of the concentration of the Austrian and Russian forces, and might induce Prussia to join the coalition. It was to his interest to dictate terms of peace after the defeat of his enemies, and not agree to any terms before then.

On this day Lannes was on the Ipps near Neumarkt.

Soult at Amstetten.

Bernadotte at Steyer.

Davout at Gaming.

Marmont at Weyer.

Murat's cavalry reached Molk.

Ney operating in the Tyrol.

The Austrian column under Merveldt, which had marched up the Enns as already related, was caught between Davout and Marmont at Mariazell and cut to pieces in attempting to regain St Polten; only a broken remnant escaped to Gratz.

Kutusoff now had only 35,000 men, so gave up all idea of defending Vienna. On the night of the 8th he crossed the Danube from Mautern to Krems, destroying the wooden bridge there after completing his passage, his intention being to effect a junction with the second Russian army under Buxhowden at Brunn, which he could reach four days sooner than had he marched to Vienna. The Russian passage of the Danube was covered by the Austrian cavalry, which then went on to Vienna.

Napoleon, by the formation of Mortier's Corps on the left bank of the Danube, appears to have expected some movement on that side; but he had placed Mortier in a dangerous situation.

Napoleon left Linz on the 9th November, and established his headquarters at Molk.

He had directed Murat to push on to the Wienerwald, unless he was resisted in force; Soult followed in support, with the other corps marching in rear.

On the 10th November Murat was at Siegharts Kirchen.

Lannes passed St Polten.

Soult was on the Traisen, with a division at Mautern.

Bernadotte was at Amstetten.

This day Mortier, on the left bank of the Danube, drove back some outposts, and with Gazan's division took up a position in the defile of Durrenstein, his other divisions being a day's march in rear. Mortier appears to have paid little heed to the enemy. He used up all his cavalry away on his left flank watching the Bohemian passes. He had neither advanced nor flank guard.

Napoleon does not appear to have heard of the Russians having crossed the Danube until the 11th November, when we find him blaming Murat for pushing on ahead, regardless of this circumstance, which should have induced him to ask for fresh instructions. Napoleon wrote to him:

> You do not weigh your orders. The Russians, instead of covering Vienna, have re-crossed the Danube at Krems. This circumstance should have made you understand that you should not act without new instructions. Without knowing the enemy's plans, or my wishes, you continue to rush my army on to Vienna. Yet you were ordered to pursue the Russians with your sword in their ribs. It is a curious way of pursuing them to move away from them by forced marches.

He told Murat to occupy Tulln and reconnoitre to his front. He now realised Mortier's danger, but too late. As soon as he reached St Polten he called Soult up, and directed Davout to halt at Modling. But Kutusoff had perceived Mortier's isolated situation, and on the morning of the 11th, advancing with Miloradovich's division from Stein, attacked him in front. Mortier counter-attacked, and drove the Russians back, but at this moment Dokhturoff's division, which had been despatched to Weisskirchen, closed the rear of the Durrenstein defile; Miloradovich was reinforced, and Mortier, surrounded by 25,000 Russians, had to cut his way out and rejoin Dupont, who arrived too late to relieve him. In this battle Gazan's division was almost annihilated.

After his defeat, Mortier recrossed the river at Spitz, with the aid of the flotilla, leaving Klein's dragoons to reconnoitre on the left bank. Napoleon now perceived that Kutusoff could either retreat into Moravia or march down the left bank of the Danube and hold the bridge at Vienna. He accordingly directed Murat to go on and seize the Vienna bridge, pass the Danube with part of his cavalry and Lannes' division, to be followed by Soult, less two divisions to remain in Vienna in reserve, and cover the route with cavalry. If he could not force the bridge, or if it had been destroyed, he was to pass at Tulln or Klosterneuburg.

Murat entered the Austrian capital in the early morning of the 18th November. Vienna had been pusillanimously abandoned by the Austrians, whose emperor had proceeded to Brunn to join the Emperor Alexander of Russia, who had arrived there with second Russian army. Only a detachment had been left at the northern end of the great Floridsdorf bridge to blow it up when the French advanced.

While Napoleon was at Linz, the Austrian Emperor had made overtures for an armistice, as already related. On the 12th November a messenger arrived in Napoleon's camp with reference to these negotiations. Murat took advantage of this circumstance to deceive the Austrians at the bridge into the belief that an armistice had been concluded. Accompanied by Lannes and Bertrand he walked along the bridge, and managed to bring some of his troops up to seize it. Although the bridge was ready for demolition, its destruction was thus prevented, and the Austrian detachment withdrew towards Brunn.

Murat pushed on, followed by the infantry, and reached Stockerau the same evening; the Russians were no longer on Napoleon's flank, where, as the Emperor said on the 11th, he had no intention of leaving them. Kutusoff had already left Krems and retreated to Ebersbrunn. Napoleon this day crossed the Danube and at midnight reached his troops. Finding that the outposts were not satisfactory he enunciated a tactical principle in his orders:

> One must always assume that the enemy has moved at night in order to attack at daybreak.

To Bernadotte he wrote on the 13th:

> The enemy has three courses open to him: (1) to move to Bohemia; (2) or to Moravia; (3) to concentrate at Krems. The last is so absurd that it is only taken into consideration as a possibility. There would be no supplies, as he is not master of the Danube. He would find himself surrounded by the entire French army, of which he knows the strength. But the probabilities are that he is already on the march.

Bernadotte was directed to cross the Danube at Krems, and to pursue the enemy; the other corps would co-operate. He would have to construct a bridge, as the Russians had destroyed the wooden structure after crossing the river on the 8th November.

It is interesting to note the distances marched by the various corps. Lannes and Soult marched 152 miles in thirteen days; Davout, 180 miles in sixteen days. These marches were generally over bad roads, cut up by the movements of the retreating enemy, or by country roads, and during or after bad weather.

On the 14th November Napoleon entered Vienna with the Guard, and established his headquarters at the palace of Schonbrunn. The Russians had reached Meissau; the garrison of Vienna, 13,000 strong, after giving up the Floridsdorf bridge, had retreated to Weikersdorf. Soult followed when relieved by Davout in the afternoon. The French line of communications had greatly lengthened, necessitating many detachments, some of which held all the passages over the Danube from Ulm to Presburg. Ney was operating in the Tyrol; Augereau was at Ulm to keep watch upon the Prussians, who had formally joined the Coalition under the terms of the Treaty of Potsdam concluded on

3rd November. Marmont was at Leoben to guard the rear from any advance from the direction of Italy and the Tyrol. Lauriston commanded detachments holding the line of the Inn.

Napoleon had directed Murat to press on in pursuit of the Russians. He hoped to destroy Kutusoff's force before it joined the second Russian army under Buxhowden, which was now approaching Brunn. But in any case, in view of the general situation, he resolved to bring the enemy to battle. Seeing the necessity for concentration, he directed Ney to leave the defence of the Tyrol to the Bavarians, and to march to Salzburg. The Austrians had already been driven out of the Tyrol, and events had occurred there, and in the Italian theatre of war, which will be related in the next chapter. Davout was to place Friant's division on the Presburg road, and Gudin's division at Neustadt, to connect with Marmont. His remaining division, now commanded by Caffarelli in place of Bisson, wounded at Lambach, was posted on the road to Brunn.

Murat, under pressing orders to try to head off, or at least inflict some damage on, Kutusoff, pushed on on the 15th, having Lannes and Soult in support, as well as Caffarelli's division. On the 14-15th the Russian had made a night march over the mountains to Schrattenthal, with a view to retreating by Jetzelsdorf on Brunn. To cover this movement he sent Bagration with 8000 men to take up a position about Hollabrunn. Murat came up with this detachment at Schongraben, but allowed himself to be drawn into negotiations for an armistice, an *aide-de-camp* of the Russian Emperor being employed by the enemy for the purpose. Thus Murat, instead of attacking, although he had no authority to act in this respect, concluded an armistice and sent back information to Napoleon. In the agreement the French were to halt, and the Russians to march out of Germany as soon as Napoleon's approval had been obtained. This was, of course, just what the Russians wanted to gain time. On receipt of this news on the morning of the 16th, Napoleon at once wrote to Murat:

I cannot express my displeasure. You only command my

vanguard and have no right to agree to an armistice without my orders. You lose the fruits of a campaign. End the armistice at once, and attack the enemy. Inform him that the general who has signed this treaty has no power to make it, that only the Russian Emperor has the right; whenever the Tsar ratifies the agreement, I also will ratify it. But it is only a ruse. March, destroy the Russian army. You are in a position to take his baggage and artillery.

Murat at once pressed forward with his cavalry and four divisions of Soult's and Lannes' Corps. Bagration had withdrawn a little and occupied a defensive position about the village of Grund, his guns posted to sweep the road from Hollabrunn, his cavalry on either flank. Here the Russian infantry fought with that stolid valour for which they have ever been and still are famous. Pressed back from Grund, they gave way slowly, fighting and in good order retiring to a second position. Here the contest was renewed, and it was not until nearly midnight that the remnant of Bagration's 8000 men, reduced to some 3000 after a fight of three to one, were beaten from the field of battle, and cut their way through the enemy, who was closing in on every side. But they had gained their object, in covering the retreat of Kutusoff's main body.

Napoleon came up next morning, and pushed on in pursuit. The cavalry reached Znaim, and was followed by Soult, Lannes, Caffarelli and the Guard, which arrived there on the morning of the 18th. Bernadotte, who had only succeeded in crossing the Danube at Mautern on the 15th, was also coming up; reinforced with a Bavarian division, he was ordered towards Budweis to hold back the Archduke Ferdinand, who was in Bohemia with 15,000 men. Mortier, after his defeat at Durrenstein, had recrossed the Danube and reached Krems. Beaumont was holding the Vienna-Brunn road with his dragoons. Klein's cavalry watched the passes to Bohemia. Napoleon gave his troops a day's rest at Znaim, writing to the Austrian Emperor that he did so out of consideration for the presence of the latter at Brunn. But no doubt the necessity for giving his men repose was the real reason for the halt, although there was no need to tell the enemy this. Very properly, it was not his custom to show consideration for his opponents in such circumstances.

On the 17th Kutusoff had reached Pohrlitz, and the remnant of Bagration's rearguard was at Fraisnitz. At Pohrlitz the Vienna garrison joined the Russians, and on the 19th Kutusoff effected a junction with the second army under Buxhowden at Wischau, some twenty miles north-east of Brunn; a few days later the allied forces under the two emperors concentrated at Olmutz.

That day the Grand Army continued the advance. Murat got to Brunn; Lannes and the headquarters to Pohrlitz, and Soult beyond that place, on the right flank. Bernadotte was at Budweis. Mortier was directed to march two of his divisions to Vienna, leaving Dumonceau at Krems. There he would relieve Davout, who would then occupy Presburg. On the 20th November Kutusoff fell back to Prossnitz, Murat advanced to the Santon, pushing the enemy's advanced posts back to Wischau, and Napoleon established his headquarters at Brunn.

It will be observed that Napoleon advanced from the Lech in three great columns, which made good the passage of the Isar and the Inn successively. On the left, Lannes marched on Braunau; Murat, Soult and Davout on Muhldorf in the centre; Bernadotte and Marmont, along the foothills, on Salzburg. His left flank was covered by the Danube, and the rear-guard echeloned on that side moving on Passau. The right column guarded the approaches from the Tyrol, where also Ney was to operate. Augereau held the line of the Lech—the advanced base. Arrived on the Inn, he established a new base, and the fresh advance to the Traun and the Enns was made on a narrower front—the left on Linz, the right on Vocklabruck.

This narrowing of the front was rendered necessary by the nature of the country, and the possibility of battle. The Emperor throughout acted on his principle: "Separate to live, gather to fight." Later, as his flank became exposed to an advance from the valley of the Muhr, Marmont covered the flank on the Styrian Alps. His troops closed in as St Polten was approached, for there was a fine position where the enemy might be expected to give battle. The advance on Vienna from beginning to end; the boldness combined with care for his communications and his flanks, the turning of the enemy on each defensive position on the successive rivers—these movements furnish a fine example of the manner in which such operations should be carried out. The boldness of his policy and his strategy in view of the attitude of Prussia has already been dealt with. There are, however, one or two points that require critical examination.

First, there is the detachment of Mortier's Corps to the left bank of the Danube, resulting in its partial destruction at the battle of Durrenstein. Detachments are, generally speaking, undesirable; and we may be sure that Napoleon would not have detached this force had he not considered it necessary to watch the passes from Bohemia. This especially in view of the fact that it was his habit, and one of his most invariable principles, to collect every available man for battle. For, as he himself said: "No force should be detached on the eve of battle, because affairs may change during the night, either by the retreat of the enemy or by the arrival of large reinforcements which might enable him to resume the offensive, and render your previous dispositions disastrous."

He was expecting the enemy to make a stand at St Polten. That he looked to the left bank of the river is, moreover, evident from his establishment of a flotilla, which should have formed a means of communication with Mortier. It may be accepted, then, that it was necessary to have a force on that bank. The fault which resulted in Mortier's defeat lay in the first instance with Murat, who was either unaware that the Russians had crossed the Danube at Mautern or, if he knew of it, did not send back information to the Emperor. In any case Murat should have kept touch with the enemy, and should have followed them closely to Mautern, and engaged their attention instead of leaving them free to deal with Mortier. He seems to have been anxious only to push on to Vienna. Mortier's defeat was due largely to his own faulty tactical dispositions. He had no advanced guard to speak of, and no flank guard; his forces were divided, one division being a day's march in rear, and he took up a bad position in a defile, where he was liable to be surrounded. It may be said that he had not expected to meet with the Russians, but he came on their outposts, and should then have taken up a strong position and called in his other division.

He here violated two principles of war; the first thus expressed by Napoleon: "An army should be ready every day, every night, and at all times of the day and night, to oppose all the resistance of which it is capable." The second, that a force should be concentrated when it is possible that the enemy may be met with, for every man is wanted in battle.

Napoleon's situation at Linz, so far from the front, until the 8th November, is open to criticism. But it must be remembered that he had the affairs of an empire as well as operations over a vast theatre of war to direct. Moreover, in too close proximity to an enemy a commander is liable to have his attention distracted by minor issues. He was, it will be observed, negotiating with the Austrian Emperor, and may have wished to protract these negotiations and so gain time and keep the enemy in uncertainty. This object would be assisted by his remaining far back from the front.

Kutusoff conducted his retreat with skill, and his rearguard actions were well and manfully fought, as were those by the Russians in Manchuria a hundred years later. The Russian general was sufficiently strong to resist the demands of the Aulic Council that he should make a stand on the Inn or the Enns with his inadequate force. Divided command caused Merveldt to detach himself and court the destruction which overtook him. There can be no doubt that the Russian was right in refusing battle until sufficient forces had been concentrated. Had he stood for the defence of Vienna with an inadequate force both the battle and the capital would have been lost. He recognised, as did Napoleon, that no geographical point, not even the capital of a country, but the enemy's army, is the proper objective in war.

This cannot be too clearly recognised, for in our own time a general has said that he had "thought the war was over because he had taken the enemy's capitals." Napoleon very rightly saw that, although he had taken the enemy's capital, it was no time to negotiate; he must defeat their armies in the field. While Murat was to blame for entering into an unauthorised armistice with the Russians, this event would not have occurred had Napoleon been nearer the front. Bernadotte's dilatory movements were also partly responsible for the escape of Kutusoff.

CHAPTER 6

Operations in Italy and the Tyrol

While the opposing armies are facing one another at Brunn and Olmutz, it will be convenient to glance at the secondary theatres of war in Italy and the Tyrol, and review the progress of operations in those countries.

It has been related how Massena commanded some 50,000 men in Italy, whose role was to "contain" the Austrian army under the Archduke Charles. The two armies stood on either side of the Adige, which, under the terms of the Treaty of Luneville, formed the boundary between Austrian and Italian territory. Neither commander seemed anxious to take the initiative. The Archduke preferred to hold Venetia rather than attempt the conquest of Lombardy, especially as he overestimated the strength of his opponents. Massena, in standing on the defensive, was fulfilling his role of holding the Austrians.

Thus a truce continued until the 18th October, when Massena attacked and took the half of Verona that lay on the Austrian side of the river, and pushed his advanced posts towards Caldiero. The Archduke fell back to the Caldiero position, with his left on that place and his right on Colognola. This was the position held by the Austrians under Alvinzy prior to the battle of Areola in 1796, of which Jomini says:

> The heights of Caldiero are the spurs of the mountains of Sette Communi, which slope gradually to the Adige, and cross the post-road from Verona to Vicenza. These heights, steep and covered with vineyards, guarded on one side by

the river and on the other by the lofty mountains from which they spring, form one of the most remarkable of military positions.

In these positions the armies remained facing one another until the 28th October, when Massena heard of the capitulation of Ulm, and sent two of his divisions to turn one each flank of the Austrians, while the others were kept in reserve in the centre. But the Archduke Charles, who had received orders to retreat on Vienna, decided first to take the offensive and strike a blow to check the pursuit. On the 30th October he attacked the French left, but the Austrians were pushed back on Colognola. Massena's right at Combine also held their own; but although a vigorous attack was made on the Austrian position at Caldiero, the French were eventually forced back on Verona when the Archduke's reserves came up. Either side had lost some 6000 men.

The Archduke now decided to retreat. On the 2nd November he fell back towards the Brenta, and crossed the Tagliamento on the 8th. Massena followed, leaving Gouvion St Cyr, arrived from Naples with 20,000 men after the conclusion of the treaty with that state, to lay siege to the large Austrian force in Venice. A series of rearguard actions was fought, but the Archduke retreated to Laybach without much loss, and on the 26th November joined the Archduke John at Marburg. Massena halted on the Isonzo on the 16th, but pressed on on receiving orders from Berthier, dated 22nd November:

> The intention of the Emperor is that you pursue the enemy without halting. Leave a corps of observation before Venice and another before Palmanova, and pursue the enemy with your sword in his ribs so that he may not be able to attack us, as we are now in the presence of the whole Russian army.

Late in November Massena passed Tarvis, and on the 29th descended the valley of the Save to Laybach, where he got into communication with Ney, on the Drave, and with Marmont.

While these events were taking place, a campaign was in progress in the Tyrol. The Archduke John took command of the Austrian forces in the Tyrol in the middle of October. Reduced by reinforcements sent to Ulm and Italy, his army now amounted to some 18,000 men, in addition to the Tyrolese militia. Of these Jellachich had 6000 in the Vorarlberg, at Lindau and Hohenembs, whither he had retreated just before the capitulation of Ulm, as related in a previous chapter. In the valley of the Inn there were 9000 men, under St Julien and Chasteler, between Kufstein and Scharnitz; and the Count de Rohan, a French *émigré*, commanded 3000 between Landech and Fussen.

The advance of the Grand Army necessitated the evacuation of the Vorarlberg and the Tyrol, and the Archduke attempted to concentrate his forces at Innsbruck with a view to retreating down the Inn to Radstadt, to support the flank of the main army on its way to Vienna. Chasteler's column of 4,000 men reached Radstadt; but the operations of the French obliged the Archduke to change his plans and retreat southwards across the Brenner Pass.

This was early in November. In the meantime Ney had reached Innsbruck on 5th November, and Augereau had entered the Vorarlberg. This combined advance made it difficult for the Archduke to clear the Tyrol. His forces were divided. Jellachich was surrounded, and surrendered to Augereau at Hohenembs on the 14th November. The Archduke retreated down the Puster Valley to Klagenfurt, where he arrived on the 20th, but de Rohan was unable to join the main body, and attempted to escape to Venice. On the 19th he got to Trent, and on the 23rd captured Bassano. But he was surrounded at Castelfranco by St Cyr, who was besieging Venice, and was compelled there to lay down his arms next day.

In the meantime Ney had crossed the Brenner Pass to Brixen, where he turned down the valley of the Drave in pursuit of the Archduke John. But the latter was already far ahead. On the 26th he joined the Archduke Charles at Marburg. From there the combined forces fell back towards Hungary, when Marmont occupied Leoben, as related in the last chapter, but were unable to rejoin the main army before the battle of Austerlitz. Their combined forces now numbered 80,000 men. They reached Komorn on the Danube, forty miles below Presburg, on the 6th December.

The faulty strategy of the Allies, which sent the Archduke Charles with the main Austrian army to Italy, has already been noted. Napoleon's rapid march on Vienna rendered useless the skilful retreat of the Archduke towards the capital. The Grand Army was already interposed between him and the Allies in Moravia before he could possibly reach the Danube.

The Austrian forces remaining in the Tyrol were too weak to be able to effect anything after the fall of Ulm. Had the Tyrolese militia been well organised, in good time, the country might have proved more difficult to conquer, as was seen later by the patriotic resistance of the people under Andreas Hofer in 1809. In this connection Napoleon's dictum, "without the aid of a regular army national risings are easily suppressed," is interesting. The evacuation of the Tyrol released Augereau's Corps for service on the line of communications of the Grand Army.

Night before Austerlitz

Chapter 7

The Battle of Austerlitz

Comments Napoleon arrived in Brunn at 10 a.m. on the 20th November 1805. A review of the whole theatre of war revealed the situation as follows:—

Position	Corps	Divisions	
	The Guard		5,300
Brunn	Lannes	{ Oudinot, Suchet }	12,000
Austerlitz	Soult	{ St Hilaire, Legrand, Vandamme }	26,000
Znaym and Budwitz	Bernadotte	{ Drouet, Rivaud, Wrede's Bavarians }	19,000
Pohrlitz		Caffarelli	6,000
Wischau	Murat	{ Nansouty, d'Hautpool, Walther }	4,500
Nicholsberg		Friant	6,000
En route to Presburg		Klein	1,000
Bohemia		Baraguey	4,500
En route to Znaym		Bourcier	2,000
Presburg	Davout	Gudin	8,000
Vienna	Mortier	{ Dupont, Gazan }	6,000
Neustadt		{ Beaumont, Dumonceau }	2,000 / 4,500
Leoben and Gratz	Marmont	{ Boudet, Gruchy }	9,000
		Total	115,800

79

The distances of these places from Brunn is about—Pohrlitz, 18 miles, Znaim, 37 miles, Budwitz, 35 miles, Nicholsberg, 30 miles, Presburg, 80 miles, Vienna, 70 miles, Neustadt, 95 miles, Leoben, 145 miles, Gratz, 155 miles. As the Allies were forty miles distant, it may be said that Napoleon had in hand for battle about Brunn and Austerlitz all troops within that range, about 75,000 men; while he could collect another 20,000 within four days. Or, if he considered that he was not strong enough to fight a battle, he could retire a few marches, call in his detachments and have the whole force above detailed at his disposal. The Allies, with the Emperors of Russia and Austria, had now assembled at Olmutz, some forty miles from Brunn. In Bohemia the Archduke Ferdinand was collecting 15,000 men, but these would be kept in check by Bernadotte and Baraguey d'Hilliers.

Ney had cleared the Tyrol, and the Archduke Charles was retiring before Massena, as already related. The Archdukes Charles and John effected a junction of their forces, 80,000 strong, at Marburg on the 26th November, but they were far distant from the decisive point; Massena and Ney were following them, and were at Laybach and Botzen on the 29th and 21st November respectively. Napoleon's communications with Vienna, and beyond that to the Rhine, were well protected. The only event to be feared in that direction was hostility on the part of Prussia. But the French Emperor was aware of the weak and vacillating character of the Prussian King. He also knew that the Prussian army could not be ready to take the field for some weeks. In case of defeat, Napoleon need not retire through Vienna. He could retreat by the right bank of the Danube, calling in his detachments to join him on the march. In view of the general situation, that has been detailed, it is obvious that the best thing for him would be an early battle.

The Allies immediately opposed to Napoleon were in superior strength. They had 80,000 men, increased to some 90,000 when the Grand Duke Constantine arrived with the Guard on the 25th November. But by a policy of delay they might hope for the arrival of the Archduke Charles and the strategical assistance of the Prussian army. But the Archduke Charles would have to march through Hungary.

The courses open to them were to attack Napoleon; to threaten his line of communications in the hope of obliging him to retreat; to await events in their present position, or to retire, in order to gain time, and draw out the French line of communications if Napoleon advanced to attack them.

On the 21st November Murat's cavalry pushed back Buxhowden and established advanced posts at Wischau. During the ensuing few days both armies rested, the Austrians at Olmutz and Olschau; the French—Lannes and the Guard in and in front of Brunn; Soult at Austerlitz and Pratzen; Murat on the road towards Olmutz; Caffarelli between Znaim and Brunn.

During this time there was some dissension in the camp of the Allies, who were nominally under command of the Tsar Alexander, but in reality under Kutusoff. The latter wished to retreat farther towards Poland, thus to facilitate the supply of the army, a matter of considerable difficulty, and for other reasons already given. Several councils of war were held; Weyrother, who had much influence, headed the party who were in favour of attacking the French, and as he was supported by the Tsar's immediate entourage his views eventually prevailed.

No doubt the views of this party were encouraged by Napoleon's apparent desire to avoid battle. He opened negotiations, and sent Savary, his *aide-de-camp*, to the Russian Emperor, "to compliment him on his arrival with the army" and "to express his esteem and his desire to gain his friendship." Savary profited by his visit to observe the "presumption, imprudence and inconsideration" that prevailed in the military cabinet of the Allies. At the same time the Prussian minister and two envoys from the Emperor Francis came to Napoleon's head-quarters, to negotiate for peace, the Austrians hoping for more favourable terms in view of the attitude of Prussia.

But Napoleon perceived that the object of the Allies was to conceal their intentions, and in fact they began to move while negotiations were in progress. On the 27th they moved to Prossnitz, and on the 28th again advanced, Bagration driving in the French cavalry from Wischau and occupying that place. His cavalry had brought the Emperor news of the advance of the Allies, and he at once directed Caffarelli, Bourcier and Klein to come up to Brunn by 7 a.m. On the morning of the 29th Bernadotte was also called in from Iglau, to reinforce the left with his two French divisions, leaving Wrede's Bavarian division to hold the Archduke Ferdinand. Mortier was ordered up by forced marches from Vienna; Davout was to advance to Raigern, where he could support the French right in the battle which seemed imminent, and which Napoleon now, in view of the Allies' movements, expected on the 29th.

Soult was in position at Posoritz, and after issuing orders for these movements the Emperor rode over to that place, and from the heights of Austerlitz observed the movements of the allied forces. These did not indicate an immediate attack, but that evening Savary returned from a mission to Olmutz, and reported that the entire hostile army was on the march.

On the 29th November the allied army, formed in five columns, continued to advance towards Austerlitz, their right on the Olmutz-Brunn road, their left on the Littawa stream. On the right was Bagration with 12,000 Russians, and 6000 cavalry under Lichtenstein. In the centre—Kollowrath (Austrian), with 17,000 men, his own corps and Miloradovich's Russians; on the left Buxhowden had three columns of 40,000 Russians under Dokhturoff, Langeron and Pribizevski, with an advanced guard of 6000 Austrian horse under Kienmayer. The Grand Duke Constantine was in reserve with the Russian Imperial Guard, 8000 strong.

Napoleon now perceived that the Allies intended to turn his right and cut him off from Vienna. He used every means to encourage the enemy to attack; received Prince Dologoruki, the Tsar's *aide-de-camp*, at the outposts, and gave him the impression that he did not desire battle; evacuated Austerlitz and withdrew Soult to the line Sokolnitz-Schlappanitz, and drew back his cavalry.

On the 30th November the Allies' outposts advanced on their left as far as Satschan, their right being at Schumitz.

Napoleon spent the 30th November in surveying the country between the Goldbach stream, behind which his troops were posted, and the Littawa. The principal feature of this ground was formed by the heights of Pratzen, which extended from Augezd to the Santon Hill, and the valleys and slopes of which afforded good cover for the movements of troops. The summit of these heights formed a plateau of considerable extent. South-west of the Pratzen were the Satschan and Melnitz lakes, now frozen over, as was the marshy ground in the valleys. The line from the San ton Hill to the Satschan Lake obviously offered a fine defensive position, behind which the Goldbach stream was no obstacle to the passage of troops to the Vienna road. Brunn was a strong fortress, between which and Raigern flowed the Schwatzawa stream behind a wood of considerable extent, affording a second defensive position.

It may seem strange, then, that Napoleon did not occupy the position indicated, and fight a defensive battle in protection of his communications with Vienna. But he had formed a great resolve. He did not wish to fight an ordinary battle in which victory would mean merely a set-back to the enemy. He determined to gain a decisive victory. This he hoped to do by allowing the enemy to continue the turning movement which he had been observing. The turning movement in progress involved the massing of troops on the allied left, and the consequent weakening of their centre, while at the same time their columns on the march would present their flank to attack. Napoleon resolved to mass his strength in the centre behind the Goldbach stream, and at the right moment break the allied centre and then destroy their separated wings.

On the 1st December the Allies continued the movement which was to bring them into a position to turn the French right flank. Their army was still in five columns; Bagration, with 13,000 men, halted in front of Raussnitz on the Olmutz road. Dokhturoff had 8500 men on the line Hostjeradek-Augezd; Langeron was in command of 11,600 on the right of Dokhturoff, on the plateau of Pratzen; Pribizevski had 13,800 behind Pratzen, and behind him stood Kollowrath with 25,400, in front of Krzenowitz, where were the headquarters and the Grand Duke Constantine with 8500 of the Russian Imperial Guard; Lichtenstein was with 6000 horse at the foot of the Pratzen plateau, between Langeron and Pribizevski.

On the 1st December Napoleon's troops were posted on the general line of the Goldbach stream: his left on the Santon Hill, which was fortified, and strengthened with twelve guns; his right on the Menitz Lake. Lannes, under whom Caffarelli had also been placed, held the left, astride of the Olmutz road, with Suchet's division on the Santon to Girzigowitz, and Caffarelli behind him; Oudinot south of the road and in front of Napoleon's bivouac, which was on a commanding hill, between Schlapanitz and Blasowitz, now known as "Napoleon's Mount," behind which the Guard was posted, in front of Bellowitz, Bernadotte on arrival this day took up a position in rear of Caffarelli, and Murat with the cavalry was posted in rear of the left wing. Soult, drawn back from the Pratzen plateau, was in the centre between Puntowitz and Kobelnitz, behind the Goldbach, having Vandamme's and St Hilaire's divisions on the left, and Legrand's on the right between Kobelnitz and Telnitz. Davout, Friant and Bourcier reached Raigern that night.

Observing the enemy's movements during the day, the French Emperor watched the progress of their turning movement, which proceeded as he wished and expected.

In the afternoon he sent for his corps commanders, and explained to them the situation and his intention for next day. His orders were issued as follows at 8.30 p.m.:—

> Marshal Soult will direct his three divisions to be beyond the ravine (the Bosenitz stream) at seven o'clock in the morning, ready to begin the manoeuvre of the day, which is to be a forward movement by echelons, right wing leading. Marshal Soult himself will be at the Emperor's bivouac at 7.30 a.m.

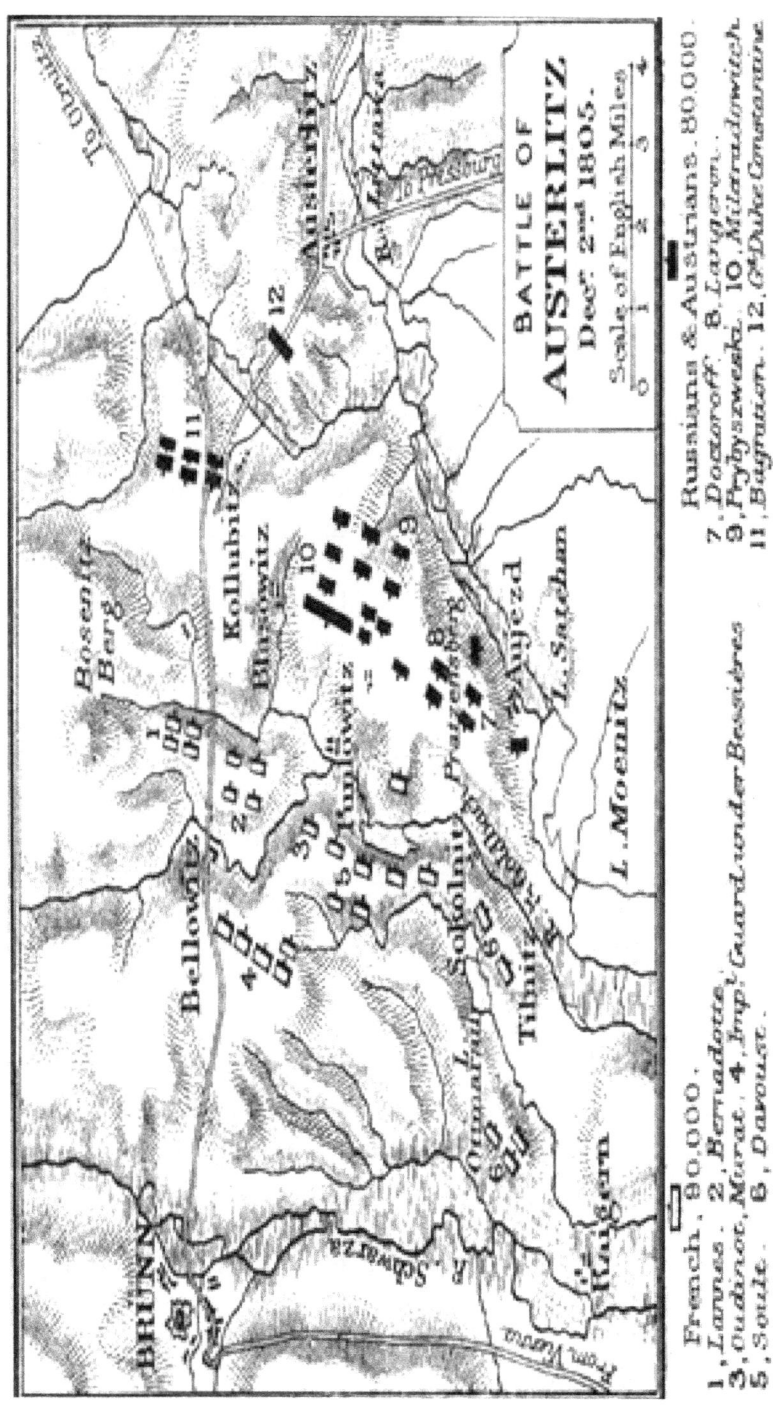

Prince Murat will order the cavalry divisions of Generals Kellermann, Walther, Beaumont, Nansouty and Hautpoul to be between Marshal Soult's left and Marshal Lannes' right at 7 a.m., to occupy as little space as possible, so that as soon as Marshal Soult advances, all the cavalry will pass the stream, and find itself in the centre of the army.

At 7 a.m. General Caffarelli will march and place his division on the right of General Suchet's division, after passing the stream. Suchet's and Caffarelli's divisions will each form two lines, a brigade in each forming one line, so that the space now occupied by Suchet's division will suffice for both divisions.

Marshal Lannes will see that Suchet's and Caffarelli's divisions are placed behind the ridge in such a manner as not to be observed by the enemy.

At 7 a.m. Marshal Bernadotte will move his two divisions into the position now occupied by Caffarelli's division, except that his left will be close to and in rear of the Santon Hill, and will remain there in column of regiments.

Marshal Lannes will order the Grenadier Division (Oudinot) to take post in line in front of his present position, the left in rear of General Caffarelli's right. General Oudinot will reconnoitre the defile where he is to pass the stream, the same defile by which Marshal Soult will have passed.

"Marshal Davout, with Friant's division and Bourcier's dragoons, will start at 5 a.m. from Raigern Abbey, and come up on Marshal Soult's right. Gudin's division will be placed at Marshal Soult's disposal when it reaches him.

At 7.30 a.m. the marshals will be at the Emperor's bivouac, when fresh orders will be given according to any movements the enemy may have made during the night.

Marshal Bernadotte's cavalry is placed under the orders of Prince Murat, who will order it to march so as to be in position at seven o'clock.

Prince Murat will similarly have Marshal Lannes' light cavalry at his disposal.

All troops will remain as above disposed pending fresh orders.

As Prince Murat's cavalry must occupy as little space as possible at first, he will have it in column.

Marshal Davout will find at the abbey a squadron and a half of the 21st Dragoons, which he will send to the bivouac.

All the marshals will give the necessary orders consequent on these dispositions.

It will be seen from these orders that Napoleon held his right weakly with Legrand's division, but that it would receive support from Davout; that his strength was massed in his centre, but hidden from the enemy, and ready for the offensive counter-stroke, which he would order in the morning according to the development of events. On his left Lannes at the fortified Santon Hill formed a strong *point d'appui*, and held the main road to Brunn.

In a proclamation read to the soldiers this day Napoleon said:

> We occupy a formidable position, and while the enemy are marching to turn my right they will present their flank to me.

At night he walked round the bivouacs, and was received everywhere with acclamations and shouts of "*Vive l'Empereur!*" while the soldiers hoisted f torches of burning straw on the tops of poles. He spent some time in observing the enemy's position, and after midnight rode over to the Satschan, to observe some reported movements of the enemy. And then he slept until dawn of 2nd December.

That night orders were issued to the allied army for next day's battle in accordance with a plan drawn up by Weyrother. Bagration was to attack the Santon Hill, the fortified post on the French left, (supported by Lichtenstein's cavalry, which was to move in the morning from its bivouac on the Pratzen plateau and deploy between Krug and Blasowitz. The Grand (Duke

Constantine with the Russian Imperial Guard would form a reserve on the allied right.

Dokhturoff was to march on Telnitz, covered by Kienmayer's cavalry, which would afterwards move in the direction of Raigern Abbey. Langeron and Pribizevski were to advance against Sokolnitz and its castle, and then, conforming to the movements of the other columns, wheel to the right to roll up the French right. This attack was under Buxhowden. Miloradovich and Kollowrath, with the allied headquarters, were to advance towards Pratzen and Pontowitz. Thus the centre of the Allies was weak. They were massed in strength on their left, and they were unduly spread out and split into isolated columns over a front eight miles in extent in order to carry out a plan which involved attack by three separate columns. Moreover, the manoeuvre was complicated in view of the position of the troops, and involved flank marches in the presence of the enemy. Briefly, the Allies would be massed on their left against the French right; the French, holding their right lightly, were in greatly superior force on their left, facing the allied right and centre.

Napoleon had already risen when the Allies began to move at daybreak on the 2nd December, and with his marshals was standing on the hill where he had bivouacked, and from whence he had a commanding view of the battlefield. The landscape was hidden by a thick fog, but these mists of night gradually cleared from the higher ground and shrank into the valleys; by seven o'clock the hilltops appeared like islands in mid-air; then the sun rose and by degrees dispersed the gathered mists. On both sides the troops in the low ground were hidden by the fog, but Lichtenstein's cavalry was seen marching towards Holubitz and soon afterwards the march of Buxhowden's masses towards Augezd, Telnitz and Sokolnitz was observed.

The battle developed exactly as Napoleon had anticipated, or, as he said, "as if both armies were performing manoeuvres under my direction." The Pratzen was soon denuded of troops as the columns moved off to the flanks, a manoeuvre not carried out without some confusion, for the various divisions had to pass each other on the march, and delay was caused by their becoming involved with one another. Preceded by Kienmayer's cavalry, Buxhowden marched his 40,000 men to turn the French right. Lichtenstein, moving off to support Bagration on the allied right, got mixed up with Pribizevski's and Kollowrath's rearguards in succession, while Pribizevski and Langeron also reached the neighbourhood of the Goldbach in some disorder.

And now on the French right the roll of musketry announced that the battle had begun. Debouching from Augezd, Kienmayer attacked Telnitz, followed the by Dokhturoff's columns, while Langeron advanced on Sokolnitz, with Pribizevski in support. Legrand's weak division could do but little against the masses of their foes; their sharpshooters were driven back across the stream and Telnitz and Sokolnitz fell into the enemy's hands. But Davout, who had marched from Raigern at 5 a.m., now appeared on the scene, and took post on the hills about Ottmarau. He attacked the heads of the allied columns as they debouched from the captured villages, and these were taken and retaken several times, until, largely with the aid of their well-posted batteries, the French re-established themselves on the line of the Goldbach and held their enemies in check.

From his commanding position the French Emperor had observed the weakness of the allied centre and the evacuation of the Pratzen heights. He asked Soult, at about half-past eight, how long it would take him to reach the heights of Pratzen, and, being told, "less than twenty minutes," said: "In that case we will wait another quarter of an hour." At about nine o'clock, seeing that the enemy's left had gone far to the flank, he gave orders for Lannes to engage Bagration in front of the Santon Hill, and directed Soult and Bernadotte to advance up the Pratzen.

These troops had been hidden in the low ground at the foot of the plateau. With Vandamme on the left and St Hilaire on the right, Soult climbed the slope and, as they reached the summit, his troops beheld, advancing in column of route, the divisions of Miloradovich (Russian) and Kollowrath (Austrian), with which were the headquarters and Kutusoff. Taken by surprise, these

Battle of Austerlitz

columns made a gallant stand; Kutusoff held Pratzen, and deployed to meet the attack; but he had no reserve, and was outnumbered and overwhelmed, largely by the fire of the French artillery, and in an hour was driven down the slope with the loss of all his guns. The remnants of the beaten columns retreated—Miloradovich on Krzenowitz, Kollowrath on Hostieradek.

While this fight was in progress in the centre, Bernadotte, with Murat on his left, between himself and Lannes, had marched on Krug and Blasowitz, while Lannes at the same time advanced upon the allied right under Bagration. Lichtenstein's cavalry, which should have formed the first line in prolongation of Bagration, had been delayed, as already related, and the Grand Duke Constantine with the Russian Imperial Guard, who was to have formed the reserve in rear of Lichtenstein, found himself in front of the latter in the first line, advancing on Blasowitz. The Grand Duke thus came unexpectedly into collision with Bernadotte, and Lichtenstein passed round his rear and came into action on his right. The Russians at once attacked, the infantry charging with the bayonet, and the cavalry riding down at the same time one of Vandamme's brigades, which was thrown into confusion, suffered heavy loss and lost an Eagle.

But Napoleon saw this reverse, and ordered Bessières and Rapp to charge with the cavalry of his Guard, which overthrew the Russians, but were in turn charged by fresh squadrons. After a combat of varying fortunes, the French horsemen remained masters of the field. Bernadotte's divisions now pushed on to attack the Russian Imperial Guard, and these were soon driven across the Littawa.

On the allied right Bagration had met with no better success; attacked by Lannes' divisions, his infantry made a fierce stand about Bosenitz, which the Russians captured. But nothing could withstand the *élan* of the French. Caught between the fire of Rivaud and Caffarelli, some Russian *cuirassiers* that had made a gallant and successful charge were swept from the field with the loss of half their number. Bagration was driven out of Bosenitz, and forced back on Kowalowitz by the weight of numbers, with the loss of his baggage and artillery. Seeing the Russians beaten, Napoleon sent to halt his left on the Olmutz road, and Lannes drew back to Raussnitz, while Bagration eventually retreated on Austerlitz.

In the meantime Soult had cleared the Pratzen plateau of the enemy; he now turned to his right to cut off the retreat of the allied left wing, still fighting on the Goldbach, advancing on Kobelnitz, Telnitz and Augezd; Drouet flanked him by moving on Krzenowitz. It was past midday, Davout and Legrand were still holding their own, and Soult's advance struck the Allies in flank and in reverse. At Kobelnitz, being surrounded, Pribizevski laid down his arms, while Langeron drew off the remnant of his troops to Telnitz.

But now the French were closing in on every side, and the Allies were penned in between the Goldbach and the Satschan ponds. Napoleon, who had seen the overthrow of Bagration on the left at about one o'clock, followed Soult with the Guard and Oudinot's grenadiers, and took post at the Chapel of St Antony. Already the battle was won, and the word to that effect passed along the French line. Buxhowden tried to break out towards Aujezd, but found his way barred by Vandamme, who pierced and cut the Russian column in two. Half the remnant, with Buxhowden at their head, broke through and reached Austerlitz with the loss of their guns; while Dokhturoff with the other half turned between the Satschan ponds. Here his troops came under a devastating artillery fire, and only a shattered remnant, skilfully and gallantly covered by Kienmayer's cavalry, made their escape into the hills to the south-east.

The battle was over. Night fell on the scattered remnants of the enemy fleeing in so many directions that their general line of retreat could not be ascertained for some time.

Never was victory more complete. The Allies had lost 15,000 killed and wounded, 20,000 prisoners, 200 guns, and the greater part of their baggage. The French loss has been variously stated at 7000 to 10,000 men.

Napoleon had watched the destruction of the enemy's left

wing from his position at the Chapel of St Antony. On the conclusion of the battle he rode over the battle-field, observing the killed and wounded. Passing through the bivouacs, he addressed each regiment; and at midnight established his headquarters at the post-house of Posoritz.

The French troops bivouacked on the line Raussnitz-Hostieradek, that had been held by the Allies the preceding day. It was too late to take up the pursuit that night, nor was it known in what direction the enemy had retreated. In fact, Napoleon himself appears scarcely to have realised the extent of his victory. But at dawn, on the 3rd, Lichtenstein came to ask for a truce on behalf, of the Emperor Francis, and Napoleon then knew that the Allies were completely broken. But his principle was not merely to defeat but to destroy the enemy. He refused a truce, appointing next day for an interview with the Austrian Emperor. He wrote to Soult:

> The Emperor will personally follow on the heels of the enemy. His opinion is that in war nothing is done so long as anything remains to be done. As long as more can be accomplished, no victory is complete. The one thing to do is to inflict as much loss as possible upon the enemy, and complete the victory.

The Allies had been obliged to abandon their line of communications with Olmutz, and had taken the road to Hungary through Goding. All troops were ordered to pursue, including Gudin's division at Nicholsberg, with the object of coming up with the enemy before they crossed the March river; and already the French troops had obtained contact with the hostile rearguards, when a truce was agreed to.

On the afternoon of the 4th the Emperor Francis arrived at Napoleon's camp, and a suspension of arms was arranged, under the terms of which the Russians returned to their country and negotiations for peace were entered upon between France and Austria, who would agree to such terms as the French Emperor imposed.

On the 26th December the Treaty of Presburg was concluded; by this treaty France received the Dalmatian provinces; the Venetian states were ceded to Italy; Bavaria obtained the Tyrol and Vorarlberg; and Baden and Wurtemburg received some accession of territory. Bavaria and Wurtemburg became independent kingdoms, and Baden a grand duchy. As an indirect result of the campaign, Prussia also came to terms, to be broken in the ensuing year, when the debacle of Jena took place. Holland and Naples became kingdoms in the Napoleonic system.

It is a trite saying that Austerlitz was the first great Napoleonic battle. In his previous campaigns the Emperor had not such numerous forces at his disposal. In the battles in Italy he had comparatively small armies: at Rivoli only 30,000, and about the same number at Marengo. It is too frequently said that, in view of modern developments, we have nothing to learn from the tactics of the past. But, though details of minor tactics change, the great principles of battle tactics remain the same, and of these the greatest is the necessity for the offensive spirit. Austerlitz is the type of modern battles, and illustrates those great principles which are recognised in our day.

It shows us that, although an army may stand on the defensive for a time with advantage, decisive success can be gained only by the adoption of a vigorous offensive at the right place and moment; and it proves that, while superior numbers have an advantage, they cannot stand against superior skill, organisation, training and moral. It is not necessary to review in detail all the lessons of this model battle; but the value of the co-operation of the three arms; of the tactical surprise which struck the enemy unexpectedly at his weakest point, and of relentless pursuit may be indicated; as also the danger of a flank march in the presence of an enemy. On this point Napoleon said:

> Nothing is so rash or so contrary to principle as to make a flank march before an army in position.

The conception of the Allies, when they had decided to attack, in its widest sense was excellent, but its execution was bad.

Austerlitz shows us that the counter-attack is the soul of defence, and that in defence, as in attack, the enemy should be held all along the line, while the decisive stroke is delivered at the favourable place and moment.

The Allies should have strengthened their centre on the Pratzen with earthworks and guns, and should have executed the earlier part of their turning movement on the previous day or night out of view of the enemy, so that it might have had in it some element of surprise. Their troops were badly posted on the 1st December, and were badly led in the battle next day. They violated Napoleon's maxim:

> It should be laid down as a principle never to leave intervals by which the enemy can penetrate between corps formed in order of battle, unless it be to draw him into a snare.

They discussed in councils of war the action that was to be taken, and, after the usual manner of councils of war, they came to a wrong decision. Prior to the battle the strategical situation was largely in their favour. They had at Austerlitz an army numerically superior to the French. Napoleon was far from his base, and his line of communications was greatly extended. It was, then, to the advantage of the Allies to have drawn him out still farther. They might well have abandoned their line of communications with Olmutz, and fallen back on the road to Hungary, where they would have been joined in a few days by the Archduke Charles with 80,000 men. They would then not only have had more chance of fighting a successful battle, but would have gained more time for Prussia to declare herself.

They had in fact everything to gain, as Napoleon had everything to lose, by delay. But the hot-heads in the allied camp who were for immediate battle gained the day, and again proved the futility of divided command, and the evils of councils of war. On this point we find in Napoleon's maxims:

> The same consequences which have uniformly attended long discussions and councils of war will follow at all

times. They will terminate in the adoption of the worst course.

As has been remarked. Napoleon might have occupied the Pratzen and taken up a regular defensive position, as an ordinary commander would have done. But by every principle of war, and especially of that great principle which makes surprise essential to success, he acted rightly. He was, moreover, m a position from which he could withdraw to another farther back, had such a course of action been necessary. It has been said that, if defeated or obliged to retreat, he would have found himself in a precarious situation with his line of communications with Vienna severed by the allied army. But that line was by no means essential to his safety. His shorter line was to retire through Znaim and by the left bank of the Danube on Passau or Ratisbon which he could have done without difficulty, favoured by the configuration of the country and by the situation of his detachments which would have conformed to the movement.

It is, perhaps, more with regard to command that tactics have changed in our day. In former times, as at Austerlitz, when even artillery ranged to no great distance, men were handled in masses by the commander on the field of battle. He was able to direct personally the manoeuvres of his troops, all of which were within a limited area almost within range of his vision. He could pass rapidly from one end of the battle-field to the other, watch every phase of the fight, and at the critical moment launch his reserve into the conflict. Thus Napoleon, posted on a commanding eminence, could survey the whole area of operations, observe the panorama-like unfolding of events, and with the unerring eye of genius could see for himself the measures that became necessary, as the battle developed, to bring about the issue of the contest. The battle lay in the hollow of his hand, and his military genius sufficed to secure the victory. The combatants were, moreover, closely engaged, and with Napoleon victory meant disaster for his enemies, who were unable to extricate their forces.

There followed the terror of the pursuit, close, pitiless, unrelenting, the whole theory of which is contained in Napoleon's instructions to Soult after the battle of Austerlitz. No hastily formed rearguard with short-ranging weapons could keep at bay pursuers who were flushed with victory. Under the conditions prevailing a hundred years ago, cavalry were in their element. Able to approach with impunity within charging distance of the foe, they could strike home with deadly effect. They completed the victory and they were pre-eminent in pursuit.

Napoleon placed great armies in the field, but the limitations of the weapons of those days led to a curtailment of the area of tactical manoeuvre. Under modern conditions, partly owing to the facilities for supply and transport afforded by railways, partly to increase of population and extension of the system of conscription, and to improvements in organisation, still larger armies are assembled in the battle area, until we find something; approaching half-a-million of men arrayed on either side. This has led to an extension of the field of battle, whilst the power of modern arms has resulted in still greater extension, both laterally and in depth.

It will therefore be easily understood that the concentration of tactical command in one person, though facilitated by the telegraph, telephone and improvements in signal- ling, is no longer possible as in Napoleon's day. The tactics of command have given place to the tactics of disposition. The commander-in-chief, under present conditions, can only dispose his troops and make known the object he desires to attain. His subordinates must therefore exercise a wide initiative; they must not be dependent on the chief as the marshals of France were on the great Emperor. They must be men of high attainments and strong character.

In one respect, however, concentration of command is as necessary as it was at Austerlitz. The battle may be won in one part of the field, but such local victory may be rendered useless by reverses elsewhere. Then it is that the commander-in-chief can influence the contest by the disposal of the great general reserve which he must have kept in his hand. In our day, as in Napoleon's time, battles are only won by reinforcing a line at the critical moment. It was at that moment which decided the winning or losing of a battle that the great master of the art of war was in the habit of using his reserves.

Austerlitz, the first great Napoleonic battle, was in some respects the precursor of the modern conflict. We find here the battle neglected by Napoleon in one part of the field in order to make the ultimate victory more crushing. Here, too, in an area of inconsiderable extent, is included a variety of physical features—hills, rivers, valleys and lakes—making the theatre of tactical operations something like a miniature of that likely to be involved in a modern battle, the vast extent of which will provide every variety of landscape.

In recent times it is with regard to cavalry and its role that controversy has been most in evidence. We see cavalry used as it should be employed throughout the Austerlitz campaign. Napoleon perfected cavalry. He separated the mounted arm from the infantry divisions and organised it in independent bodies. And although in his time almost the whole role of cavalry on the field of battle was comprised in shock tactics, he recognised the necessity of arming his cavalry with carbines. Many of his instructions with regard to the use of this arm hold good to this day. Thus:

> An army superior in cavalry will always have the advantage of being able to cover its movements, and give battle only when it chooses. Its defeats will have few evil consequences and its successes will be decisive.

It may be safely said that cavalry still has a great future before it, and that its deeds in the next European war will be no less glorious than at Austerlitz. Under modern conditions the battle is long drawn out, sometimes lasting many days. The bloody scenes of the fight are continuous; there is no wild charging and cheering of infantry amid the smoke, to sustain the spirits and fire the energies of the combatants; the horrors of the battle will be ever before them, and they will become physically and morally exhausted. But the cavalry, kept back under cover, will be comparatively fresh for the attack on exhausted infantry with both fire-arms and cold steel, according to circumstances. Woe! then, to that side which breaks and flies.

Possibly we may yet see the horrors of a Napoleonic pursuit. But effective pursuit is more difficult owing to the containing capacity of modern arms. A few rifles or guns strongly posted may hold in check a very large body of men; and a strong rear-guard thus disposed, especially if fresh troops are available for the purpose, should enable the retreat of a defeated army to be carried out comparatively unmolested.

CHAPTER 8

The Causes of Success

It has been said of Napoleon that he always defeated the enemy with numerically superior forces. Even were this true, there could be no higher praise; the fact that he overwhelmed Mack with 200,000 men exhibits the skill of the great commander who could bring such superior force into operation at the decisive point and moment. In fact, it was one of the attributes of the great commander that he always had this superiority. Even when numerically inferior, as on the field of Austerlitz, he brought a superior force to bear on the enemy at the decisive point and moment. In his tactics, as in his strategy, surprise was one of the main f actors of success.

He had, as has been indicated, the advantage of undivided command and command of the resources of the State. And, as he himself said:

> Nothing is so important ill war as undivided command; for this reason, when war is carried on against a single power, there should be only one army, acting upon one base, and conducted by one chief.

He showed his pre-eminence both as a soldier and a statesman in preparation for war, recognising the fact that such preparation is the main factor of success, for an army cannot be improvised on the outbreak of hostilities.

He fulfilled the duty of the statesman in providing the army which as the soldier he trained and led in war. In the foregoing chapters the factors of success on the one hand and of failure on the other have been generally indicated. But it seems necessary to go deeper than the mere indication of principles or events which evolved cause and effect. The achievements of Napoleon cannot be ascribed merely to his observance of certain principles, deduced from the nature of things and from a study of military history. Certainly his exposition of military art, marks an epoch in the operations of war, and it fell to him, in an age when the correct application of military principles had been forgotten, to deduce from the experience of history and illustrate in the practice of war the whole art of war, based on immutable principles and exemplified in the annals of the world.

Napoleon's very name sounds like a trumpet-call; his genius illuminates one of the most lurid and marvellous epochs in the history of the world. But it is not sufficient to ascribe his success to "genius," although in effect that was the main and primary cause. Genius must be analysed or, at least, being in itself something intangible and indefinable, it is necessary to discover the means by which it operated or found expression. In the first place we find an unbounded energy of both mind and body; a grasp of first principles, of cause and effect—a knowledge that certain causes would produce certain effects; a faculty of creating favourable situations, and of commanding the situations so created; an imperious disposition, which insisted on things being accomplished, and recognised nothing as impossible of accomplishment; a cool head, even in the most exciting situations; unequalled force and decision of character, and a mind capacious of great events.

While he had an unequalled grasp of details, and knew that the success of an enterprise frequently depends on such details. Napoleon knew also how to neglect minor matters, leaving them to adjust themselves, and to concentrate his attention on broad issues. He had, in fact, that wisdom beside which the mere term "cleverness" sounds petty and insignificant. There are many "clever" men, but few wise ones. And he had an insight into human nature which enabled him to rule men, partly by his knowledge that "there are two levers for influencing men, fear and self-interest." All these faculties constituted character, and a personality whose magnetism dominated all with whom he came into contact or who served under his command; and even now, nearly a hundred years after his death, that personality influences the minds of men and ensures him that deathless fame of which he said:

> I hold the immortality of the soul to be the memory we leave in the minds of men; it were better never to have lived at all than to leave no trace of one's existence behind.

Eminently a man on what Matthew Arnold terms "the first plane," he knew not only how to command success, but to reap the fruits of victory—the faculty of the statesman.

He possessed in the highest degree the ability of choosing subordinates to carry out his will. It has been said that "only in despotisms are men in high places chosen only for their fitness." The galaxy of talent that rose to eminence in the Napoleonic epoch is evidence of the truth of this aphorism; but other factors contributed. As Napoleon said:

> Revolutions are a favourable time for soldiers possessing courage and intellect.

Only in great political cataclysms are men of character and talent likely to find a fair opportunity of rising professionally above the general dead-level. It may be recognised, in all armies, in the words of the famous Prussian General Order of 1849, that

> it is necessary that the higher commands should be attained only by those officers who unite distinguished ability and military education with corresponding qualities of character.

But in practice, especially in times of peace, though that is the time for such appointments if we are to be prepared for war, this ideal is difficult of attainment. The general atmosphere of intellectual sterility, the dull routine of army life, the slow promotion by seniority, which generally renders it impossible for men to reach high command until past their intellectual and physical prime, under a system where mediocrity succeeds no less surely than brilliant attainments—these do not conduce to the production of men on the first plane in any rank of an army.

It is frequently said that generals are born, not made. There was even a period, not so long ago, when men who made a study of their profession were regarded as mere bookworms, and intellectual attainments were regarded as of small moment, if not as a positive disadvantage. Those days are happily past, although even now, at least in our army, the man who makes a constant study of his profession is exceptional. But while generals are not born, certainly there are attributes, inherent in some men, which are favourable to the development of military genius. These have been indicated in the case of Napoleon, of whom General Clarke, French plenipotentiary in Italy, wrote to the Directory in 1796:

> Here all regard him as a man of genius. He has great power over the soldiers of the Republican army. His judgment is sure; his resolutions are carried out with all his powers. His calmness amidst the most stirring scenes is as wonderful as his I extraordinary rapidity in changing his plans if obliged to do so by unforeseen circumstances.

But in his case, as in that of practically every great general known to history, knowledge gained by study supplemented the inherent qualities of genius. Let us see what he says himself on this point:

> Read again and again the campaigns of Hannibal, Caesar, Gustavus Adolphus, Turenne, Eugene and Frederick. Model yourself upon them. This is the only means of becoming a great captain and of acquiring the secret of the art of war.

The truth of this is exemplified in the career of Napoleon.

His subsequent campaigns were conducted with no greater skill than the campaign of Italy, in which he held his first command. His strategical conceptions were due to no inborn genius, no inspiration of the moment. They were based on the immutable principles derived from a close study of military history, which, says Jomini, rightly interpreted, is the true school of war.

Yet elsewhere we find Napoleon saying that

Generals-in-chief must be guided by their own experience. The science of strategy is only to be acquired by experience.

At first sight this dictum may not appear to agree with the preceding one. Napoleon took command of an army and exercised it with success when a young man of twenty-six with no experience of war, as experience is commonly understood; but he had what is worth more, the, experience gathered from the wide domain of history and the ability to apply it in practice. Indeed, in a lifetime the ordinary soldier can acquire but little personal experience of war, and such as he has will probably tend to limit his mental horizon and obscure his view of the wider issues of military art, unless he has also deeply studied war; just as the general who is too near the actual scene of conflict in a battle is liable to have his attention distracted by minor issues, and his breadth of vision narrowed by what is taking place before his eyes. We have seen this in our time, when we were deluged with "lessons of the war" to the exclusion of all the experience of previous history.

Napoleon himself said:

All great leaders of ancient times, as well as those who have since followed in their footsteps, accomplished great deeds only by observing the I principles of the art of war, by the correctness of their combinations and a careful weighing of means and results. They have succeeded only by adapting themselves to these principles, no matter what the boldness of their enterprises and the extent of their operations. They never ceased to make war a true science. To this extent they are our great examples, and only by imitation can we hope to emulate their deeds. The principles of the whole art of war are those which guided the great commanders whose exploits are handed down to us by history.

At the same time it must be borne in mind that the lessons of history are no guides to be followed blindly and mechanically, nor are the facts themselves of importance, but the knowledge we derive from them. Wisdom, however, does not consist in the mere accumulation of knowledge, but in the derivation of judgment from experience.

And what is experience? The personal experience of the little span of one human life is limited indeed, but we have at our command the experience of two thousand years of history. Willisen [1] wisely said regarding experience in war:

> It is true war can only be learned by experience; but what are we to understand by 'experience'? Who gains experience, the man who has been present during this or that event, but has never thought in the least about it, either before or after it or while it was taking place; or the man who has had no personal experience of such matters but who studies a great number of such wars, and who has always and everywhere examined the causes which produced the results, and learnt from them that certain results always recur if preceded by the same causes, and who has at length formulated views and deduced general principles? Has not the latter 'experience' and the former none? Shall I not by such experience alone learn to know war, whilst by the other I shall remain altogether ignorant of it?

Thus by these means we find Napoleon well versed in the art of war before he had any personal experience in the field; and

---

1. Quoted in Yorck von Wartenburg's Napoleon as a General.

Berthier unable to apply the very first principles of strategy after twenty campaigns, with the living example of the great master ever before his eyes.

But study and a knowledge of theory, however completer are not alone sufficient. The general must have also character, indomitable resolution, iron will and physical and mental vigour to carry his conceptions to a successful issue; for the ablest plans will not command success unless carried through with resolution. The pedant may make a good plan of campaign, but he will not be able to execute it. For, when all is said, man is the last, as he is the first, instrument in war. The ultimate business of war is fighting. As leaders of men we do not want mere armchair students, or those who have commanded only office files. We want men of affairs, men of action, accustomed to live a life of physical and mental activity, possessing an adventurous spirit, and having a wide knowledge of the world and of human nature. Victory may be on the side of the big battalions, but only if they are properly directed and inspired with the spirit of offensive warfare by their leaders. "The strength of an army," said Napoleon, " is estimated by multiplying the mass by the rapidity"; and the rapidity will be in proportion to the energy and enterprise of the leaders.

An Overview of the Campaign

FROM THE 18TH OF MAY, 1804,
TO THE 20TH OF DECEMBER, 1805.

The news of the elevation of France into an Empire, and the proclaiming of Napoleon as its Emperor, was received by the sovereigns of Europe with an amount of complacency plainly indicating that such an event had been foreseen, if not altogether expected. Despite the protest of the Count de Lille, the chief of the Bourbons, staying at Warsaw, and who issued a most impolitical document to all the crowned heads, calculated to alienate the sympathies of France rather than to enlist them, these monarchs, with the exception of three, acknowledged the new member of their family so strangely thrust upon them. Not out of goodwill to Napoleon himself, as may be supposed, for they could be no more indifferent to a change in the form of government of so great a nation as France than the nation herself.

Not unmindful of this feeling either in his subjects or in the foreign Powers, Napoleon gave the former reasons for assuming his new dignity, which silenced and disarmed, if they did not destroy all opposition. He also made a pretence of sacrificing the Republic in order to allay the alarm of the absolute monarchs. If he imagined that they believed in this attempt at homogeneity, he was mistaken. They might hold out their hands in simulated friendship, but from the bottom of their hearts they knew that he was but a military *parvenu*, whom it was their interest to conciliate nay, even to support in his usurpation, rather than risk the prolonging of a state of revolution which could be but a bad example to their own peoples. In this way the European Courts silently watched each other as to which should take the initiative in congratulating the new Emperor. The King of Spain was the first, and curiously enough, the Cardinal de Bourbon, Archbishop of Toledo, added his officious congratulations to those of his sovereign.

The King of Prussia followed suit, and sent a most flattering message to Napoleon. Austria, double-dealing as usual, and in secret intelligence with the British Cabinet, stood aloof for a little while. She approved of the transforming of the Republic into an hereditary monarchy, but raised an objection to the title of Emperor, though she assured the Trench Ambassador, who rather haughtily responded to these expostulations, that they arose neither from ill-will against his master, nor from any regard to the manifesto of the Count de Lille, of which she in common with other Courts had taken no notice.

The difficulty was simply that the dignity of Emperor of Germany had been till now elective, and Francis II feared that, if the title departed from him or his successors, they would no longer be on an equality of rank with the ruler of France, unless he himself adopted this title for his hereditary states. To this objection Napoleon made a very gracious answer, and Francis having proclaimed himself Emperor of Austria, hastened to acknowledge Napoleon as Emperor of the French.

Russia not only refused to acknowledge the new title of the house of Austria, pretending that it was a plot concocted between Francis II. and Napoleon, but by going in mourning for the Duke d'Enghien, and by various demurrers as to the violation of the Baden territory in connection with the late prince's murder and France's interference with the kingdoms of Naples and Sardinia, sought a pretext for war with Napoleon, and recalled her ambassador.

Of this situation Francis, secretly inclining to Alexander I., and rendered somewhat bold by the conciliatory attitude of Napoleon in the late negotiations with regard to the Imperial dignity, sought to take advantage. Gustavus IV., of Sweden, the quixotic champion of the legitimacy of the Bourbons, imitated Russia's example, and declared himself the most stubborn enemy of France. This declaration Napoleon answered in the *Moniteur*, by saying that he looked upon the King of Sweden as a young fool, with whom he should be sorry to confound a brave and loyal nation.

He assured them of the continued goodwill of France, promised that their merchant vessels should always be well received in her ports, and that Sweden's fleet might even revictual and repair there if it liked. This rendered Gustavus more enraged, and a note of the Swedish Minister, in which the Emperor was called Monsieur Napoleon Bonaparte, informed the French *charge d'affaires* at Stockholm of the cessation of all relations between the two Governments. Already more than half influenced by England, Gustavus now signed a subsidiary and commercial treaty with the Cabinet of St. James's (7th September).

In England, the rupture of the Treaty of Amiens, an event scarcely expected so soon by Napoleon, had entailed the fall of the Addington Ministry, pledged to peace, as it were; and Pitt and his party resumed the direction of affairs, exciting the nation to hostilities by pretending to show that peace was a greater obstacle to her commercial prosperity than war. England's interests were supposed to be threatened by Napoleon's avowed intention to close the Continent to British trade; a reprisal, as the Emperor argued, for the arbitrary proceedings of England in connection with all maritime affairs.

The whole war now took an aspect of unexampled ferocity, degenerating into personal calumny, as well as into the most unheard-of piracy, scarcely creditable to the admirals of civilised governments. English and French papers continued to vilify each other's rulers; and a pamphlet appeared in England, written by the Rev. Edward Hankin, which openly preached the destruction of France, whose existence was shown to be incompatible with the prosperity of England. Moreover, the English declared all French ports in a state of blockade, and prevented all neutrals, from Fécamp to Ostende, from entering, whilst their cruisers chased every ship they could see, and took even several members of the Emperor's family as prisoners to England.

No state was allowed to remain outside the strife. Spain, which, as we have seen, had redeemed by a sum of money her obligation to furnish a contingent to Napoleon, was importuned by the English Cabinet, after it had acknowledged the transaction, to come over to her side, and, unable to comply with the prescribed conditions, was openly attacked at sea, notwithstanding all absence of a declaration of war. Four Spanish frigates coming from Rio de la Plata, and containing more than a million pounds sterling, were summoned to surrender, and upon their refusal, an engagement took place, in which one of the Spanish vessels exploded, the other three being taken to Portsmouth.

This unjustifiable act aroused the indignation of a large number of members of the English Parliament, but their protest not- withstanding, the spoliation continued in other places, the ambassadors remaining all the while at their respective courts, until Spain, feeble as she was, felt compelled to declare war against England, and signed a treaty with France, by which she placed thirty line-of-battle ships at the latter's disposal (12th December). Finding all his efforts to prevent an outbreak of hostilities fruitless, and knowing that England was trying to establish a Coalition between Russia, Austria, and Prussia the last Power, however, still standing aloof, Napoleon vigorously pushed his preparations for an invasion of the English coast.

A hundred and twenty thousand men, distributed in seven camps along the French Channel, could be concentrated in thirty hours, and embark in more than two thousand gunboats and small vessels ready for the purpose. This project, though openly propagated, served mainly to hide a more important naval operation, for despite the opinion of many, that a landing might be attempted successfully with the troops of the flotilla, Napoleon did not deem it prudent to risk the flower of his army or to venture upon a naval engagement with two thousand " nutshells." He was determined not to endeavour to cross the Channel, save protected by a strong fleet, composed of ships now lying forgotten in the various French ports, but which were stealthily being put in commission with the utmost activity.

The great enterprise, to be accomplished with the co-operation of the Dutch and Spanish fleets, was to be entrusted to a brave and bold sailor, Latouche-Tréville, in whom Napoleon had great confidence, and who was to command the fleet of Toulon, in addition to being appointed Inspector-General of the Mediterranean coast. "Give us but the mastery of the Straits for six hours, and we will be masters of the world," he wrote to the latter.

Pending these preparations, and his own coronation, Napoleon made several journeys in the interior in order to consolidate his new power. He started from Paris on the 18th of July for Boulogne, where he passed in review the troops, stimulating them by his presence, and distributing several Crosses of the Legion of Honour, then recently instituted. He inspected most minutely every arsenal, depôt, and wharf, and was also an eye-witness of an engagement, which the English began, thinking to profit by a violent storm that overtook the French ships, and wherein the former were scarcely successful. From thence he visited all the camps and ports situated on that part of the coast, and returned to Paris to celebrate his birthday, on which occasion there were national *fêtes* throughout France.

Meanwhile, public institutions for the furthering of arts, sciences, and literature, in accordance with the Emperor's views, were founded under his protection. He visited, accompanied by the Empress, the four departments on the left bank of the Rhine, showing himself interested in the manufactures and industries, reorganising municipal and local affairs, planning high roads, canals, and various improvements favourable to commercial and sanitary welfare. By these means, while rendering his position more secure in the interior, he sought to inspire his foreign enemies with a dread of his importance in the exterior.

However secure Napoleon might pretend to be with regard to his new Imperial dignity, he wanted to render it more stable still by an appeal to the people. The nation sanctioned his title by an overwhelming majority. There was now but wanting one formality, prescribed by the *Senatus Consultus*, which had raised him to the throne: the oath to the constitution by the Emperor in presence of the great bodies of the State and the high dignitaries.

This ceremony Napoleon wished to convert into a coronation. The most ancient chronicles were ransacked to find examples for the pomp and splendour with which the Emperor wanted to invest it. He even wished it not to take place in Paris, ostensibly because the Parisians had not shown themselves sufficiently indignant at the late attempts upon his life, in reality because he feared their ridicule and discontent at the proposed splendour and consequent expenses. In remembrance of the feasts of the Federation, the Champ de Mars had been proposed; but the Emperor refused to be crowned there.

Several members of the Council suggested that the ceremony should be celebrated in the church of the *Invalides*, as this fane would appeal more to the military enthusiasm, and be free from all the monarchical and religious traditions attached to Notre Dame, still somewhat repugnant to the scarcely slumbering spirit of the Revolution. But though Napoleon first selected the *Invalides*, in concession to the anti-religious tendencies of the people, he finally chose the latter for the very reason of its sacred associations in relation to the coronation of kings. This religious impression, for which he himself could have cared but little, was necessary, he imagined, to impose upon the peoples and kings. He wanted to be consecrated by the Pope, and consequently overtures were made, almost before the *Senatus Consultus* had proclaimed him Emperor, to induce Pius VII to come to Paris to perform the ceremony.

At first the Pope refused for various reasons, principally because he would not consecrate the usurper of a throne to which there was a legitimate pretender. Yet the Pontiff's reluctance may be more justly ascribed to the wish of enhancing the price of this favour, and by these means to obtain once more possession of the Legations, Bologna and Avignon, of which Napoleon, even before his accession, had deprived him. Nor is there any doubt that Napoleon lulled him with this hope, though, while doing so, he had already secretly resolved to transform these same states into a Kingdom of Italy, and assume himself the iron crown of the Lombardian Kings.[1]

However, by dint of promises and threats, Pius was prevailed upon to come, while Josephine, enjoying but a doubtful reputation, and only civilly married to Napoleon, went through the religious part of the marriage ceremony, which was secretly performed by the Cardinal Fesch, the Emperor's uncle.

About the middle of November the Pope reached the end of his journey, and was met by Napoleon, dressed as if he were out hunting, a few miles from Fontainebleau, whence they entered a carriage and arrived at the castle, being welcomed by thunders of artillery and the military presenting arms. A few days later, the whole Court removed to the Tuileries, where the Pontiff was installed in the Pavilion of Flora, and received the congratulations of the high dignitaries, and notably of the Senate, in his private apartments.

All this while the Pope had never doubted but that he would. place the crown on Napoleon's head, and that the latter would publicly partake of the Holy Communion. The Emperor flatly rejected both proposals, Pius being secretly rejoiced at the refusal of one, knowing full well that its acceptance would have been tantamount to sacrilege.

Still fostering the greatest hopes as to the result of his journey, the Holy Father showed himself anxious to please in every respect, going even as far as to propose the canonisation of a certain Bonaventura Bonaparte, a distant relative of the Emperor, and who died many years ago obscurely in a cloister. "Holy Father," answered Napoleon, "spare me this ridicule. As you are in my power, people would not fail to say that I had compelled you to provide a saint in my family."

The preparations for the coronation being completed, each performer's part in the ceremony having been carefully re-

---
1 Michelet, *Histoire du XIX. siècle*, vol. 3., bk. 2., ch. 6.

hearsed, [2] the coronation took place on the 4th of December, with a pomp and splendour unsurpassed, and scarcely equalled, by anything in modern history.

This magnificence notwithstanding, the people, attracted by the novelty of the spectacle, remained cold and indifferent, only condescending once to depart from their stolidity at the sight of a priest on a broken-down hack, in the suite of the Pope, the two appearing like a comic interlude in a vastly serious play.

"I, who was on the Boulevard (I was six years old)," says M. Michelet, "I noticed nothing on that ice-cold day, save a gloomy and dispiriting silence." [3]

Nor did any of the subsequent festivities make the people relax in their cool and silent indifference to the new state of things. Without openly expressing their discontent, save in the isolated case of one individual, [4] the sight of all this theatrical show, so foreign to their recent Republican institutions, made them feel that this was not the wished-for culmination to fifteen years of constant sacrifice of wealth and life.

They had hoped to find in Napoleon the worthy military chief of a Republic, who would in no way remind them of the senseless etiquette of the *ancien régime,* so distasteful to the masses; now they saw, more "in sorrow than in anger," that he, like the kings of old, would be separated from the people by a crowd of dignitaries and courtiers. They regretted that nearly five million *francs* should have been spent in aping the ceremonies of courts, against which they had of late so energetically protested, the more so as the transition of a Republic into an Empire had been signalised by several fiscal and monetary changes, entirely to the disadvantage of the poorer classes.

2. These rehearsals took place, some openly in the gallery of Diana, and others secretly in the private drawing-room of the Emperor, on a large table, by means of a model of Notre Dame and of wooden puppets, made by the painter Isabey, and representing in full costume all the personages, even the Emperor and the Pope.
3. Michelet, *Histoire du XIX. siècle,* vol. 3, bk. 2, ch. 6.
4. A young medical student, Faure, two days after the coronation, made a fruitless attempt to reach the Emperor whilst he was distributing the Orders of the Legion of Honour, in order to assassinate him. The attempt was regarded as that of a madman, and he was merely sent back to his parents.

It is a question whether Napoleon, in reality anxious for the welfare of the nation, in trying to impose upon others, did not in the end impose upon himself. His desire for peace led him to imagine that, by imitating the trappings of legitimate sovereignty, he might invest the new order of things with an aspect which should prove it to be in no way hostile to ancient Europe, and show at the same time an indestructible stability of its own.

Thus he thought to pave the way for an amicable settlement of all differences between his enemies and himself. With the same intentions, perhaps, he gathered around him many of the former nobles and *émigrés*. It need hardly be said that personally he cared little for their pretensions, but between them and the rest of the European aristocracy there existed a bond which might tend to alloy the bitterness felt against a usurper, and bring about a more friendly feeling, which undoubtedly was wished for by Napoleon.

Besides, if there was to be a court, it should be as graceful and refined as possible, and with his surroundings of parvenus and swash-bucklers, this was well-nigh impossible without the assistance of the ancient nobles, trained to obsequious court-service, and who did not disdain those offices which his generals and their wives would have haughtily refused. The reason of this was not far to seek; it lay in the difference of morals and manners. "The old noblesse," said the Emperor, "showed much more grace and zeal in their attendance. A lady of the Montmorency family would have rushed to tie the strings of the Empress' shoes; the wife of Marshal Lannes would have shrunk from doing this, for fear of being mistaken for a lady's maid; a Montmorency had no such fear." [5]

The hopes of Napoleon to induce his enemies to preserve peace were doomed to disappointment; and it is probable that he has been unjustly accused of wishing to wage war just then, for it was his interest not to do so; though we do not pretend to say that he may not have desired it later on. Even M. Michelet, who persistently and conscientiously attacks him, is reluctantly obliged to admit that the hatred of Pitt caused the war, rather than the vain, but, perhaps, provoking preparations for the invasion of England. It is certain that, despite the rebuff which he had already once received, when First Consul, from George III., he wrote to him a second time to put an end to the hostilities already begun.

It was a rather manly letter, [6] from which the moderate party in England conceived the strongest expectations of a lasting peace. But the forms of a representative government did not allow the king to answer, and a reply was sent (Jan. 14th) by the Secretary for Foreign Affairs, in which England asked for time to consult the Continental Powers. This was followed, three days later, by a confidential communication of the English Prime Minister to the Russian Ambassador in London, and of which the contents presupposed long anterior negotiations.

This memorandum aimed at nothing less than to make France return almost to her ancient territorial limits, and to share between the contracting Powers her conquests; a proposal which was to be the basis of the Coalition-treaty, signed on the 11th of April of the same year, between England, Russia, and, later, by Austria, despite that State's most amicable relations with the French Empire, and her recent congratulations to Napoleon. Nor were the angry and indignant remonstrances of Fox of any avail. Napoleon could doubt no longer the enmity of England and of Russia of Austria he had his suspicions, but no certainty while an attempt was made to inveigle Prussia into the alliance by the promise of Belgium, failing to comply with which demand Alexander, secretly supported by the Queen of Prussia, threatened to occupy Pomerania, in case the King of Sweden should be attacked. Nevertheless, the Prussian Cabinet resisted.

Napoleon had now no other choice left but to baffle and defeat the Coalition by fresh battles, and by the subjugation of the Continent. Driven, as it were, to acts of usurpation against the neighbouring States, in order to secure his own position, he

---

5 Las Cases, *Mémoires*, vol. 2, p. 332.
6. Letter to the King of England, 2nd January, 1805, in the Napoleon Correspondence.

began by altering the Constitution of the Batavian Republic according to a less democratic model, though probably he considered this but a provisional state of things, previous to annexing Holland to France, so as to be more fully protected against hostile attempts from that side. For this reason the supreme government of Holland was entrusted to a Legislative of twenty members, and the executive to a Grand Pensionary, elected for life. Schimmelpenninck, who was chosen for this office, was entirely devoted to the interests of France (May 30th).

In Italy, things were dealt with more summarily. This country had borne the name of a Republic for three years, during which time her Constitution had worked smoothly; and though Napoleon, as President, disposed of an almost absolute power, he did not much abuse it, thanks to the sensible influence of the cool-headed Vice-President Melzi. To defy England and terrify Austria, Napoleon now prepared to have himself crowned King of Italy, stipulating at the same time, in deference to the national susceptibilities of the Italians, that after his death none of his successors should wear the crown of Italy united to that of France.

The Emperor had offered the Italian crown to his brother Joseph; but the latter, for various private and political reasons, saw fit to refuse. The coronation of Napoleon took place at Milan with great splendour (26th May). The Pope, who had been invited to be present, declined, scarcely satisfied with the results of his journey to Paris, of which he had entertained great expectations, which were not realised. The vice-royalty of Italy was entrusted to Eugène Beauharnais, Napoleon's stepson, whom he intended to be his successor, an article in the new Constitution giving the King of Italy such a right of selection from among his male issue, legitimate, illegitimate, or adopted.

The State of Genoa, lately known by the name of the Ligurian Republic, had sent a deputation, headed by the Doge, to the coronation of the King of Italy. It was received with all honours as the embassy of an in- dependent people, but no one imagined that Napoleon had the intention of incorporating Genoa with the newly-erected kingdom, the more so as he had always stipulated for and respected its independence. Lately, however, there had been signs that a secret influence was at work to induce the Genoese themselves to propose this incorporation, under 'the pretext that as an independent Republic they were not sufficiently powerful to protect their coasts against English aggression; and although the Austrian Ambassador, who saw through the scheme, disliked it, and protested, the deputation who had come to Milan beseeched Napoleon to unite to his empire this "Liguria, the first theatre of his victories, the first step of the throne on which he was now seated, and to grant them the happiness of becoming his subjects" (4th June).

In an answer which accorded with their expressed inability to protect themselves, the Emperor accepted, and the Ligurian Republic was divided into three departments, and provided with a reconstructed Constitution, based as usual on the French model. About the same time, he erected Piombino, ceded to France in 1801, into a principality for his sister Eliza, while the Republic of Lucca, re-enacting the fable of the frogs, asked the Emperor for a ruler belonging to his family and for a new Constitution, both of which were granted, Prince Baciochi, the husband of Princess Eliza, being selected for their ruler. Parma, Piacenza, and Guastalla, hitherto under their own particular laws, were now also provided with new Constitutions, and incorporated to France, according to the new Imperial system.

During his triumphal and pacific journey through Italy, on which the eyes of all Europe were now turned, Napoleon had not lost sight of his chief aim, the war with England. He was aware of the doubtful attitude of the other powers, of Austria, arming under many specious pretexts, and of the threatening symptoms of a new Coalition. "While it was believed in France and even in England that all these great preparations for invasion were but so many scarecrows, Napoleon, amidst the various occupations, necessitated by the great reforms he was accomplishing in the interior, found time to be in daily communication with the Minister of Marine, Decrè, who alone possessed his confidence, since the death of Latouche-Tréville at the end of

1804. Far from abandoning his idea of invading England, he had conceived a new strategic plan. The admirals of the Toulon, Rochefort, and Brest fleets, Villeneuve, Missiessy, and Gantheaume, were each to set sail for the West Indies, land reinforcements, and then return together suddenly to Europe, while the English would despatch their ships to succour their threatened colonial possessions. Then, when the French admirals should have come back safe, they would be masters of the Channel, and might prove the truth of the words Napoleon never ceased repeating, "Give us but the Channel without the English fleet for six hours, and England shall have ceased to exist."

In fact, though the scheme did not succeed, it at least caused one of the English admirals, Nelson, to be seeking for Villeneuve in Egyptian waters, whilst the latter eluded his vigilance, and arrived safely at his destination. Having received information on his arrival that Missiessy had already been there and returned, and that Gantheaume could not appear because he was blockaded in Brest by Admiral Cornwallis, he was instructed to set sail for Martinique and afterwards for Corunna, to meet there fifteen Franco-Spanish ships of the line, and with these to start for Rochefort, join Missiessy's squadron, relieve Gantheaume still locked in, and then to enter the Channel with the combined fleets.

Villeneuve was to take the supreme command, and to steer for Boulogne, where Napoleon himself would await him. If they could be but masters of the Channel, wrote the Emperor, there would be no difficulty in landing a hundred and sixty thousand troops on the English coast. Everything had been prepared, every adverse chance foreseen and guarded against. If Villeneuve found it impossible to raise the blockade of Brest without giving battle, he was to begin an engagement as near as possible to that port, in order that Gantheaume might take part in it; if insuperable obstacles prevented him from entering the Channel, the fleet was to repair to Cadiz, to occupy the Straits of Gibraltar, to ravage its roadstead, and to re victual.

Such were the last instructions to Villeneuve, and from them may be seen that Napoleon had almost provided against and for everything to assure his descent on the English coast.

Unfortunately, Villeneuve was not the man to enter fully into the spirit of such a vast enterprise, nor had he the genius to execute it. Of this Napoleon became fully aware a few days after Villeneuve had started, when he received a dispatch from the admiral, in which the most puerile events were magnified. He there and then resolved to appoint Gantheaume, still lying at Brest, and wrote to dismiss Villeneuve from his command, and to let the fleet, under Gantheaume, sail to her appointed destination.

While Villeneuve was slowly making for Ferrol, wasting time in capturing unimportant merchant vessels, Nelson had followed him to the West Indies, where he only arrived to learn the departure of the foe of which he was in search. Penetrating the design of Napoleon, he cautioned the Admiralty, who commanded the concentration of the different fleets, the very thing which Napoleon had wanted Villeneuve to do. It is worthy of notice, that in the letters to his Minister of the Navy, Napoleon, commenting on the news received from London, foretold, as it were, the decisions which the situation would inspire in the lords of the English Admiralty. Be this as it may, Nelson was ordered, as Napoleon had foreseen,[7] to reinforce the squadron before Brest; and the fleet cruising before Rochefort, under Admiral Stirling, was to join that at Ferrol, commanded by Sir Robert Calder.

The French flotilla and the army which it had to transport being in readiness, and the Dutch fleet, fighting along the whole of her route, having also arrived at Ambleteuse, near Boulogne, Napoleon himself returned from Milan. Nothing was wanting now but the naval forces, whose appearance upon the scene was hourly expected. Beginning to grow uneasy about the fleet of Villeneuve, of whom he had no tidings, and strongly preoccupied by the turn affairs were now taking on the Continent, he started for Boulogne, resolved to await there the arrival of the

---

7. There is a letter to this effect in Napoleon's Correspondence, dated 20 *Prairial*, Milan, addressed to his Minister of the Navy, Decrès.

fleet, without whose assistance he dared not cross the Channel.

He hoped that the report of his meditated invasion would be sufficient to keep the Continent in respect,—for Austria was massing her troops on the Inn and the Adige,—and that the reverses of England would prevent all further Coalition.

In case his enemies, profiting by his absence, should begin hostilities on the Rhine, he calculated to have his expedition terminated before then, and to be back in France to oppose an invasion of the Empire. He sent word to Gantheaume to hold himself prepared, because Villeneuve could not fail to appear shortly. In fact, he thought that the missing admiral, informed of Nelson's pursuit, might have steered for Cadiz instead of for Ferrol, in which case every precaution was already taken to assist him.

After waiting for three days, during which he reviewed the army in sight of the English cruisers, he received the news that Villeneuve, with a very superior force, had fought an engagement with the united fleets of Admirals Stirling and Calder, about sixty miles to the westward of Cape Finisterre (July 22nd); that both parties claimed the victory, but that two Spanish line-of-battle ships had fallen into the enemy's hands.

Instead of following his orders, and trying to join the squadron of Rochefort, Villeneuve wasted another two days, and then entered Ferrol, and with thirty ships of the line allowed himself to be blockaded by twenty vessels. Napoleon was indignant that one man should have upset all his plans. In the midst of his anger, his thoughts immediately reverted to the Continent, where lie thought to strike England in her Allies, and he sketched out a campaign, which subsequent events proved to have been one of the masterpieces of military strategy.

Nevertheless, he still hoped that Villeneuve would manage to break the blockade, and sent him orders to do so. He was to make for Brest, where Gantheaume would attempt an engagement and join him. The Emperor was, indeed, loth to abandon a plan which, notwithstanding its difficulties, was likely to be successful, for while awaiting for further news he tried the forces of his flotilla by a bolder movement than had hitherto been attempted. This movement answered all his expectations, and made the more bitter his regret at being so inefficiently supported by his admirals.

According to his orders, Gantheaume left Brest harbour to offer battle to the enemy, expecting Villeneuve to come to his succour. The latter had, indeed, left Ferrol, but instead of steering for the north, he remained in the Ferrol roads, afraid of the responsibility, and then finished by running into Cadiz, where he was blockaded by the united fleets of Calder and Collingwood, of which Nelson had taken the command.

When the news of Villeneuve being unable to appear reached Napoleon, he knew that his great projects against England had vanished. In less than four-and-twenty hours the whole army was directed on Germany, to punish Austria, which was going to pay for England. As may be seen, Napoleon's plan of an invasion of England was far from being intended as the mere scarecrow which some historians have so persistently maintained it to be.

In order to understand the subsequent events, we must retrace our steps for a few months to the time when Napoleon left for Italy to be crowned at Milan.

On the very day of Napoleon's departure (11th April), a treaty, the result of long negotiations, had been signed between England and Russia, aiming principally at, and ostensibly compelling France to restore the European equilibrium, to despoil her of the advantages which she had obtained by fifteen years of incessant war and bloody sacrifices, and to isolate her from the rest of Europe, with which, since the Revolution, and especially now, she had nothing in common.

England engaged to support these demands by co-operating with Russia, by furnishing her naval and military forces, by subsidising every other Power which should league itself with her to the annual amount of 15,000 for every ten thousand men supplied in return for which subsidies she was to be considered the chief of this third Coalition, and to have the right of establishing commercial depôts in the States of her Allies. At the same time all her pretensions on the sea were recognised.

Another article accorded similar monetary advantages to the King of Sweden, who had openly joined the Coalition. As for Austria, Alexander sent his *aide-de-camp* to Vienna to discuss the plan of the campaign, and despite the assurances of the French Ambassador that the camp of Alessandria was dispersed, that the one of Brescia would share a similar fate within a fortnight, Francis continued to mass his troops upon the Italian frontiers, though he was too double-dealing to declare war at once, thinking that the time had not yet arrived.

To give the Coalition leisure to complete its preparations, and to assemble its forces, the farce of a pretended negotiation was attempted in which Alexander should play the part of mediator. Prussia was also invited to enter the Coalition, Its king was in a critical position. Scarcely confident of being able to maintain his neutrality, he had hoped all along that actual hostilities should be prevented.

Suddenly, undeceived by the, appeal of the Russian Ambassador in favour of his master, he fell into his former irresolution, aggravated on one side by his ambition, on the other by some political motives, which made him loth to refuse the bait held out to him by France in return for his alliance, namely, the cession of Hanover; while at the same time he dreaded the aggression of Russia, in case he should by accepting this offer appear to lean to Napoleon's side. In this emergency he pursued a double-faced policy, by declaring his wish to remain neutral, merely consenting to take Hanover as a depôt, free, as he thought, to side afterwards with the Power who should prove the stronger.

Meanwhile the preparations for war on the part of the Coalition continued with redoubled energy, especially on the part of Austria, who on the reiterated demands of Napoleon, threw off the mask at last, and clearly showed that the drift of her supposed mediation was to gain time in order to complete her plans. She declared that the violation by Napoleon of the Treaty of Luneville, one of whose articles stipulated and guaranteed the independence of the Italian as well as of the Helvetian and

Batavian republics, had led her to enter the Coalition.[8] She still professed herself willing to re-open negotiations, but this also was done in order to gain time and to obtain the alliance of the Electors, who of late had become important princes, and on whose attitude much depended in the coming campaign. In this instance Napoleon, however, had been too quick, and forestalled her, especially with the Electors of Bavaria and Baden, who could not possibly remain neutral in the struggle, though, above all, the first desired to do so.

This Elector expressed this wish to the Emperor Francis, but saw it daily disregarded by the invasion of his territory by Austrian troops, eager to reach the Rhine before Napoleon had broken up his camp near Boulogne. Napoleon had foreseen this, and extracted a promise that in case such an event should happen, the Bavarian army would seek refuge elsewhere, and effect its junction with his army. The Austrians having passed the Inn on the 9th of September, the Elector gave the order for his troops to enter Franconia, and abandoned his capital to transfer his Government and himself to Wurtzburg, where a treaty with France was definitely arranged on the 23rd of November, much to the disgust of Austria.

The troops of the Boulogne camp crossed France by forced marches, and in three columns, making for the Rhine by parallel roads. Germany was to be the theatre of the war, the French Emperor having resolved to act merely on the defensive in Italy. The army in Italy, only fifty thousand strong, was entrusted to Masséna, supported by the troops which were evacuating the Naples territory, after the king had signed a treaty of neutrality, and promised to prevent the landing of foreign troops. Napoleon himself having taken various measures for the due government of the interior, and for the levy of conscripts, joined his troops, who had already passed the Rhine (24th September).

Bernadotte, commanding the first corps, had evacuated Ha-

---

8. According to some French authors this was a mere pretext, sufficiently proved by the fact that Austria had entered the Coalition before the changes in the existence of the Italian Republics had happened.

nover, merely leaving there a garrison, and joined the electoral troops at Wurtzburg; the second corps, under Marmont, left Holland, and was moving on Mayence; four corps under Davoust, Soult, Lannes, Ney, and a reserve of cavalry under Murat, starting from Boulogne, were stationed along the Rhine from Mannheim to Strasburg.

Another corps, under Augereau, moved from Brest upon Huningen, as reserve. There were a hundred and sixty thousand troops in all, exclusive of the Bavarians. Murat and Lannes crossed the Rhine at Kehl, threatened the issues of the Black Forest, and masked the movements of Ney, Soult, and Davoust (25th September). The following day Ney crossed near Lauterburg, Soult near Spires, and Davoust near Mannheim, the three marching on the Necker, to intimidate the Electors of Baden and Wurtemberg, whom they induced to sign treaties, whereby they secured sixteen thousand electoral troops to guard their communications.

Marmont crossed at Mayence, and joined Bernadotte and the Bavarians at Wurtzburg, so that in two days a hundred and eighty thousand men were stationed in *échelon*, on the right flank of the Austrians, facing Lannes and Murat, in the Black Forest, whose lines extended towards Stuttgard, where they joined those of Ney. Mack, the Austrian general, in reality directed and browbeaten by the Austrian princes, who treated him with contempt on account of his inferior birth,[9] understood nothing of all these complicated movements. Counting upon the Russians, who were expected hourly, he lost his head at the enemy's rapid marching and countermarching, and mistaking their intentions, he found himself outmanoeuvred, his supports beaten on all sides, and compelled to enter Ulm.

Being summoned to capitulate, he ultimately agreed to surrender if he was not relieved within eight days. In the meantime the news spread that a division of Austrian troops who still kept the field before Mack had entered Ulm, had surrendered at

---

9. Michelet, *Histoire du XIX. siècle*, vol. 3, bk. 3, ch. 4.

Trochtelfingen, with the exception of two thousand horsemen under the Archduke

Ferdinand, who had made good their escape. A part of the French army had marched a hundred and thirty-five English miles in five days, had killed or made prisoners twenty-two thousand Austrians, taken a hundred and thirty guns, and a large number of *caissons* and wagons. The French Emperor sent this news to Mack, who immediately surrendered with thirty-three thousand prisoners, sixty cannon, and forty standards (20th October).

Well might the world stand astonished at the spectacle of an army of eighty-five thousand men destroyed, as it were, without one great battle having been fought. Well might the French soldiers say, "The Emperor has beaten the enemy with our legs, and not with our bayonets." They were proud of their general, and not without reason. For two days the rain had fallen in torrents, the troops were drenched to the skin, they had received no rations, they were up to their knees in mud, but their sufferings and privations were shared by Napoleon, as if he had been the meanest private.

As he was standing in their midst, a batch of Austrian prisoners passed, and a colonel expressed his surprise that the Emperor of the French should be covered with mud and exhausted with fatigue like the humblest drummer in the army. One of his *aides-de-camp* having explained what the Austrian said, Napoleon sent him back the following answer, "Your master has reminded me that I was once a soldier; I trust that he will acknowledge this time that the purple has not made me forget my previous occupation."

One would have thought that after the crushing lesson inflicted upon Austria, Prussia would not have courted the risk of a similar defeat, and, if departing at all from her professed neutrality, would have sided with France. She did the very opposite. In their rapid march from Wurtzburg to the Danube, Marmont and Bernadotte had entered the Prussian State of Anspach. The King of Prussia showed himself very indignant at this, and declared that henceforth he was free from any engagement with France. This was probably a pretext, as the same thing had happened before without the least notice being taken; but Alexander took advantage of this. He proposed an interview to Frederick William, and arrived unexpectedly at Berlin on the 25th of October, five days after the capitulation of Ulm, when the full extent of the disaster was not known. He was received with the greatest warmth, the two monarchs embracing each other amidst the loud applause of the people.

At Potsdam, where the illustrious guest was entertained, there was nothing but festivities, exchange of presents, and of congratulations. From that moment France was utterly disregarded. The French Ambassador, already recalled by Napoleon, took leave of the King of Prussia on the 1st of November, and on the 3rd an offensive and defensive treaty was signed, by which the king entered the Coalition, though he still reserved the right of withdrawal, in case Napoleon should consent to the evacuation of Holland and Switzerland, grant an indemnity to the King of Sardinia, and separate the crowns of Italy and France. An ambassador was despatched with this ultimatum, who took care not to arrive at the French head-quarters until a month after the signing of the treaty at Potsdam.

The key to the above-mentioned reservation is to be found in the tidings of the disaster at Ulm, communicated by the Austrian Archduke Anthony, two days before the signing of the treaty, and which tempered the warlike ardour of the Prussian Court and Cabinet. Nevertheless, the alliance was cemented in a somewhat theatrical performance arranged by the Queen. The two monarchs went at night to the tomb of Frederick the Great, where Alexander swore to die for the honour and defence of Prussia.[10]

Despite Napoleon's willingness to explain the passing through Anspach, the Prussian army was mobilised, Hanover invaded in the name of the Elector-King, and every preparation made to enter upon a campaign.

---

10. Hardenberg, *Memoires*, vol. 9, pp. 14, 55, quoted by Michelet.

Meanwhile Napoleon, resolved to strike terror into the hearts of his enemies, was rapidly invading the Austrian provinces, scarcely meeting with any resistance either from the Austrians or from the Russians, who had now arrived, and were retreating upon Vienna to protect the capital, and to give the armies of the Tyrol and Italy the opportunity of joining them.

The French troops under Ney and Augereau, who were left behind, were ordered to invade the Tyrol, to drive out the Archduke John, and to cover at the same time the right flank of the army of Germany as well as the left of the Italian army. The Inn, totally undefended, was passed by all the French corps; Braunau, one of the great victualling depôts of the Austrian Empire, taken without a blow; whilst Lannes and Murat, forming the vanguard, drove the enemy successively from their various positions. Kutusoff, the Russian general, finding it impossible to effect a junction with the armies of the Tyrol and Italy, abandoned the plan of defending Vienna, and retreated into Moravia, where he hoped to meet the second Russian army.

Scarcely had he reached the other side of the Danube before he was attacked by Marshal Mortier, sent thither to watch Bohemia, and who had but a small contingent under his command, the remainder of his division being a march behind. Nevertheless, the French took the offensive, ignorant of the exact numbers of the enemy until too late, when they found out the superiority of the Russians by being completely surrounded at nightfall and their retreat cut off. From assailants they became defenders until the remainder of their division came up, when the Russians, taken between two fires, were compelled to fall back on Krems. This engagement is better known under the name of Dürrenstein, the village near which it was fought (11th November).

The Emperor Francis and the Court had left Vienna and taken refuge at Brunn, in Moravia. From there they started for Olmütz, where the Emperor of Russia, with his second army, was stationed. The Austrian capital was a prey to the greatest confusion. One day the most confidential reports as to the ultimate success of the war were circulated, the whole population being called under arms to ensure this success; the next the treasures, the archives, and valuables were hastily packed up, and an embargo laid upon every boat to remove them into Hungary.

Meanwhile an envoy was sent to Napoleon to propose an armistice; a proposal which the latter declined, saying, that at the head of two hundred thousand victorious troops, he could not very well grant an armistice to a beaten army. The French continued their way to Vienna, which city they merely passed through, and marched straight to the great bridge over the Danube, which led across that river to the northern provinces of the Empire.

That bridge was mined and watched from the other side by fourteen thousand Austrians under Count Auersberg, who had orders to blow it up on the least attempt at violence. On the Vienna side of the river there was only an outpost. In this emergency Lannes and Murat bethought themselves of a stratagem. They tried to persuade the Austrians that the armistice of which there had been rumours afloat for the last few days was actually signed.

Two French generals were the first to arrive on the bridge at the head of the 10th Hussars; they demanded to speak to the German commander, and were allowed to pass, but alone. Some French soldiers followed and halted, whilst Lannes and Murat dismounted, and with a small detachment passed on to the bridge. General Belliard, as if taking a stroll, advanced also, his hands behind his back; Lannes joined him; they were gaining ground notwithstanding the objections of the captain on duty.

These were seemingly unnoticed, and two or three French officers engaged him in conversation and talked about the armistice. He, however, was losing patience, and when he saw the detachment advancing still farther, he began to rally his men; but Lannes and Belliard took hold of him and shouted louder than he. The dispute was waxing hot, the moment critical, when the French troops quickened their pace, crossed the remaining distance, reached the other side, and made themselves masters of those who were to fire the train. Auersberg had been duped, and was summoned before a council of war, deprived of his rank and dignity, and condemned to a year's confinement in a fortress.

The Suchet division and the grenadiers of Oudinot crossed also; the light cavalry immediately continued their advance, in order to impede the march of the Russian general, Kutusoff, the same who had been defeated by Mortier, at Dürrenstein; Soult followed; Bernadotte had passed the Danube at Mautern, while Davoust occupied Vienna. Kutusoff, knowing that Bernadotte was in his rear, is said to have sent a flag of truce to Murat in the name of the Czar, and to have escaped by means of a pretended armistice with the French general.

When Murat, aware of the deception, and severely reprimanded by the Emperor, resumed his march, he found that the whole of the Russian army had defiled rapidly in his rear, and that only a corps of ten thousand troops had remained stationary. A sanguinary engagement ensued, but the Russians offered a stout resistance, which, gave their general time to reach Brunn (18th November).

The Allies, aware that the war was assuming a new aspect, ordered the Archduke Ferdinand to raise an insurrection in Bohemia, while his army should cover the left flank of the Russian troops and the remainder of the Austrians, who had effected their junction at Brunn. The Archduke Charles re-crossed the Alps, entered Hungary, and was thus enabled to protect the Austro-Russian contingent on the right.

This Archduke had been scarcely more fortunate in Italy than his fellow-generals in Germany. When Austria first resolved to join the Coalition, she intended to carry the war into Italy, while merely remaining on the defensive in Germany. In furtherance of this plan, approved of by her Allies, she had despatched thither a numerous army under the Archduke, who had instructions to invade the newly-created kingdom the moment the Russians should appear on the Inn. We have seen how this intention was frustrated by the rapid advance of the French on the Rhine, but Napoleon, who intended to remain on the defensive in Italy, and had taken his measures accordingly, emboldened by his first successes on the Rhine, also changed his tactics, and ordered Masséna to take the offensive, mainly to prevent the reinforcements which Charles might send into Germany. Acting upon this, Masséna attacked Verona, and the *tête du pont* at Legnago, carried them both after a violent engagement (17th October), crossed the Adige, and followed the Archduke, who had entrenched himself at Caldiero.

Another engagement took place, in which the Austrians maintained their positions for three days, though with a loss of four thousand killed, whilst the French lost as many (30th October). When the news of the defeat of Ulm arrived, the Austrians precipitately retreated towards the Alps. Masséna, still at their heels, failed for some days in bringing them to a standstill to offer battle.

The Archduke, harassed and fatigued, wishing to give his troops some rest, threw four battalions of grenadiers and some field artillery into Vicenza. After a fruitless summons to surrender, Masséna resolved to take that town, and being unsuccessful, contemplated to resume the attack the next day; but the Austrians evacuated the place during the night, having accomplished their aim, namely, to give time for the artillery and the wings of the army to join the centre.

Masséna pursued them, without being able to force them to give battle, until he arrived at the right bank of the Tagliamento, where the Archduke, after throwing a garrison into Venice, made a stand in order to cover the march of his baggage-wagons on Palma-Nova. A serious engagement took place, a repetition of which was again avoided by the Archduke, who crossed the Julian Alps, concentrated his troops at Laybach, and there awaited the junction with the army of the Tyrol in order to march to the assistance of Vienna.

Masséna was not in a position to follow him, as troubles had broken out afresh in the Kingdom of Naples, where the queen, disregarding the treaty entered into by her husband, had invoked the aid of the Anglo-Russians, and placed an army of twenty-five thousand troops at their disposal, with which the Roman territory was to be invaded. Without communication with the grand army, unaware of the taking of Vienna, of the operations of Ney and Augereau on his left, of the position of the Archduke John, uneasy at the reported arrival of the Anglo-Russians in Dalmatia and in Naples, Masséna deemed it wiser not to venture too far, and contented himself by sending out strong reconnoitring parties, and by making himself master of Trieste. The corps which on the conclusion of the treaty with Naples had left that kingdom was employed to invest Venice.

The troops under the Archduke John, after remaining for some time idle in the Tyrol, held in check by Ney, and harassed in their retreat by a detached brigade of Masséna, had managed to join the Archduke Charles at Cilly, whence both endeavoured to get to Vienna by way of Hungary and the Danube, in this way to harass the flank or rear of the French, and join the Russians in Moravia. But Marmont going to their encounter, compelled them to make for the Raab, while Davoust, possessing himself of Presburg, and forcing the Hungarian Diet to remain neutral, opposed a formidable barrier in front; Masséna, having passed the Alps, harassed their rear.

Meanwhile Napoleon had moved his head-quarters into Moravia, as far as Brunn, the Russians having retreated to Olmütz. At the moment when another great battle was to be fought, a war contribution of forty millions of *francs* was levied on Austria, Moravia, and the remainder of the conquered provinces, whilst one of the same amount had already been paid before. The stores of the Austrian arsenals which could not be used were sold, and their proceeds distributed among the French army in the shape of three months' extra pay to every general, officer, and soldier who had been wounded in the present war.

After several days passed in pretended negotiations, tacitly encouraged by Napoleon, who wished to gain time in order to discover the blunders of his enemy, the Allies took the offensive on the 27th of November by driving the Trench outposts from Wischau, and executing a movement towards Austerlitz, which betrayed their intentions of cutting off the French from Vienna, whither, however, the latter had no thought of retiring. The military movements of Murat, Lannes, and Soult were mistaken for retreats, and the Russians continued their tactics to cut off the French communications with the Danube.

Napoleon left them in their error to attract them to the spot chosen by himself, which was the plateau of Austerlitz. He succeeded in this; for the Russians, fearing that the French army should escape them, slowly left their positions, and executed a flank march in column, by which they attempted to turn the right flank of the enemy. From that moment Napoleon was certain of the victory. "Tomorrow, before nightfall, that army will be mine," he said.

On the 2nd of December the battle began. The Allies commenced the attack by carrying the village of Sokolnitz; but the French troops, under Soult, stormed the heights of Pratzen, and after a desperate conflict of two hours' duration, the allied army was pierced through the centre, and its left wing entirely separated. The Russian right was also completely defeated, by Bernadotte, Murat, and Lannes, with the loss of nearly half their number. At last, after a tremendous cavalry encounter between the Russian Imperial Guard and the French Cavalry of the Guard, the Russians gave way and retreated. The loss of the Allies was immense. Thirty thousand men were killed, wounded, or made prisoners; a hundred and eighty pieces of cannon, four hundred caissons, and forty-five standards fell in the hands of the conquerors. Napoleon might well say to his brave troops, "I am satisfied with you; you have covered your eagles with immortal glory."

The consequences of this victory were very great. Two days after a personal interview between the Austrian and French Emperors (December 4th), an armistice was concluded, which was ratified three weeks later at Presburg, and by which it was stipulated that the French were to occupy all those portions of Upper and Lower Austria, the Tyrol, Styria, Carinthia, Carniola, and Moravia, at present in their possession; that the Russians should return to their own country; that all insurrectionary movements in Hungary and Bohemia were to be stopped, and no armed force of any other Power should be permitted to enter Austrian territory. The Russian

Emperor was allowed to retire with his troops by slow march, but renewed the war later on, so that Napoleon said of Alexander, that "he was as false as a Greek of the Lower Empire." The King of Prussia sent an envoy to compliment Napoleon on his victory, and signed a treaty with the latter by which he ceded to France the Margravate of Anspach and the principalities of Neufchâtel and Cleves, for which 'he received in return the Electorate of Hanover. The King of Naples, who had assisted the Coalition by placing his army on a war-footing, under the direction of a Russian general, was to be dethroned, and Joseph, Napoleon's brother, was some time afterwards appointed King of the Two Sicilies (March 30th, 1806).

But whilst the French were triumphant on land, the English gained a naval Austerlitz. The French admiral, Villeneuve, wishing to retrieve his reputation, and being in command of thirty-three line-of-battle ships and five frigates, attacked the English fleet, composed of seven-and-twenty ships of the line and four frigates, under Nelson and Collingwood, a few leagues to the north-west of Cape Trafalgar (October 21st).

The result was that nineteen large French or Spanish vessels were taken, of which five afterwards escaped to Cadiz, sixteen were either wrecked, burnt, or sunk, and only four arrived safe at Gibraltar, as well as three French admirals and seven thousand prisoners. By this victory England remained mistress of the sea, and had no longer any maritime rivalry to dread. It was, however, dearly bought, by the death of the great English admiral, Nelson.

Immediately after having gained the battle of Austerlitz, it seems that Napoleon intended to form three compact nations of fifteen million Italians, thirty million Germans, and fifteen million Spaniards, and to create a system of federal States to the French Empire.

ALSO FROM LEONAUR
AVAILABLE IN SOFTCOVER OR HARDCOVER WITH DUST JACKET

CAPTAIN OF THE 95th (Rifles) by *Jonathan Leach*—An officer of Wellington's Sharpshooters during the Peninsular, South of France and Waterloo Campaigns of the Napoleonic Wars.

BUGLER AND OFFICER OF THE RIFLES by *William Green & Harry Smith* With the 95th (Rifles) during the Peninsular & Waterloo Campaigns of the Napoleonic Wars

BAYONETS, BUGLES AND BONNETS by *James 'Thomas' Todd*—Experiences of hard soldiering with the 71st Foot - the Highland Light Infantry - through many battles of the Napoleonic wars including the Peninsular & Waterloo Campaigns

THE ADVENTURES OF A LIGHT DRAGOON by *George Farmer & G.R. Gleig*—A cavalryman during the Peninsular & Waterloo Campaigns, in captivity & at the siege of Bhurtpore, India

THE COMPLEAT RIFLEMAN HARRIS by *Benjamin Harris as told to & transcribed by Captain Henry Curling*—The adventures of a soldier of the 95th (Rifles) during the Peninsular Campaign of the Napoleonic Wars

WITH WELLINGTON'S LIGHT CAVALRY by *William Tomkinson*—The Experiences of an officer of the 16th Light Dragoons in the Peninsular and Waterloo campaigns of the Napoleonic Wars.

SURTEES OF THE RIFLES by *William Surtees*—A Soldier of the 95th (Rifles) in the Peninsular campaign of the Napoleonic Wars.

ENSIGN BELL IN THE PENINSULAR WAR by *George Bell*—The Experiences of a young British Soldier of the 34th Regiment 'The Cumberland Gentlemen' in the Napoleonic wars.

WITH THE LIGHT DIVISION by *John H. Cooke*—The Experiences of an Officer of the 43rd Light Infantry in the Peninsula and South of France During the Napoleonic Wars

NAPOLEON'S IMPERIAL GUARD: FROM MARENGO TO WATERLOO by *J. T. Headley*—This is the story of Napoleon's Imperial Guard from the bearskin caps of the grenadiers to the flamboyance of their mounted chasseurs, their principal characters and the men who commanded them.

BATTLES & SIEGES OF THE PENINSULAR WAR by *W. H. Fitchett*—Corunna, Busaco, Albuera, Ciudad Rodrigo, Badajos, Salamanca, San Sebastian & Others

ALSO FROM LEONAUR
AVAILABLE IN SOFTCOVER OR HARDCOVER WITH DUST JACKET

WELLINGTON AND THE PYRENEES CAMPAIGN VOLUME I: FROM VITORIA TO THE BIDASSOA *by F. C. Beatson*—The final phase of the campaign in the Iberian Peninsula.

WELLINGTON AND THE INVASION OF FRANCE VOLUME II: THE BIDASSOA TO THE BATTLE OF THE NIVELLE *by F. C. Beatson*—The second of Beatson's series on the fall of Revolutionary France published by Leonaur, the reader is once again taken into the centre of Wellington's strategic and tactical genius.

WELLINGTON AND THE FALL OF FRANCE VOLUME III: THE GAVES AND THE BATTLE OF ORTHEZ *by F. C. Beatson*—This final chapter of F. C. Beatson's brilliant trilogy shows the 'captain of the age' at his most inspired and makes all three books essential additions to any Peninsular War library.

NAVAL BATTLES OF THE NAPOLEONIC WARS *by W. H. Fitchett*—Cape St. Vincent, the Nile, Cadiz, Copenhagen, Trafalgar & Others

SERGEANT GUILLEMARD: THE MAN WHO SHOT NELSON? *by Robert Guillemard*—A Soldier of the Infantry of the French Army of Napoleon on Campaign Throughout Europe

WITH THE GUARDS ACROSS THE PYRENEES by *Robert Batty*—The Experiences of a British Officer of Wellington's Army During the Battles for the Fall of Napoleonic France, 1813.

A STAFF OFFICER IN THE PENINSULA *by E. W. Buckham*—An Officer of the British Staff Corps Cavalry During the Peninsula Campaign of the Napoleonic Wars

THE LEIPZIG CAMPAIGN: 1813—NAPOLEON AND THE "BATTLE OF THE NATIONS" *by F. N. Maude*—Colonel Maude's analysis of Napoleon's campaign of 1813.

BUGEAUD: A PACK WITH A BATON by *Thomas Robert Bugeaud*—The Early Campaigns of a Soldier of Napoleon's Army Who Would Become a Marshal of France.

TWO LEONAUR ORIGINALS

SERGEANT NICOL by *Daniel Nicol*—The Experiences of a Gordon Highlander During the Napoleonic Wars in Egypt, the Peninsula and France.

WATERLOO RECOLLECTIONS by *Frederick Llewellyn*—Rare First Hand Accounts, Letters, Reports and Retellings from the Campaign of 1815.

AVAILABLE ONLINE AT **www.leonaur.com**
AND OTHER GOOD BOOK STORES

ALSO FROM LEONAUR
AVAILABLE IN SOFTCOVER OR HARDCOVER WITH DUST JACKET

THE JENA CAMPAIGN: 1806 by *F. N. Maude*—The Twin Battles of Jena & Auerstadt Between Napoleon's French and the Prussian Army.

PRIVATE O'NEIL by *Charles O'Neil*—The recollections of an Irish Rogue of H. M. 28th Regt.—The Slashers— during the Peninsula & Waterloo campaigns of the Napoleonic wars.

ROYAL HIGHLANDER by *James Anton*—A soldier of H.M 42nd (Royal) Highlanders during the Peninsular, South of France & Waterloo Campaigns of the Napoleonic Wars.

CAPTAIN BLAZE by *Elzéar Blaze*—Elzéar Blaze recounts his life and experiences in Napoleon's army in a well written, articulate and companionable style.

LEJEUNE VOLUME 1 by *Louis-François Lejeune*—The Napoleonic Wars through the Experiences of an Officer on Berthier's Staff.

LEJEUNE VOLUME 2 by *Louis-François Lejeune*—The Napoleonic Wars through the Experiences of an Officer on Berthier's Staff.

FUSILIER COOPER by *John S. Cooper*—Experiences in the 7th (Royal) Fusiliers During the Peninsular Campaign of the Napoleonic Wars and the American Campaign to New Orleans.

CAPTAIN COIGNET by *Jean-Roch Coignet*—A Soldier of Napoleon's Imperial Guard from the Italian Campaign to Russia and Waterloo.

FIGHTING NAPOLEON'S EMPIRE by *Joseph Anderson*—The Campaigns of a British Infantryman in Italy, Egypt, the Peninsular & the West Indies During the Napoleonic Wars.

CHASSEUR BARRES by *Jean-Baptiste Barres*—The experiences of a French Infantryman of the Imperial Guard at Austerlitz, Jena, Eylau, Friedland, in the Peninsular, Lutzen, Bautzen, Zinnwald and Hanau during the Napoleonic Wars.

MARINES TO 95TH (RIFLES) by *Thomas Fernyhough*—The military experiences of Robert Fernyhough during the Napoleonic Wars.

HUSSAR ROCCA by *Albert Jean Michel de Rocca*—A French cavalry officer's experiences of the Napoleonic Wars and his views on the Peninsular Campaigns against the Spanish, British And Guerilla Armies.

SERGEANT BOURGOGNE by *Adrien Bourgogne*—With Napoleon's Imperial Guard in the Russian Campaign and on the Retreat from Moscow 1812 - 13.

AVAILABLE ONLINE AT **www.leonaur.com**
AND OTHER GOOD BOOK STORES

ALSO FROM LEONAUR
AVAILABLE IN SOFTCOVER OR HARDCOVER WITH DUST JACKET

LIGHT BOB by *Robert Blakeney*—The experiences of a young officer in H.M 28th & 36th regiments of the British Infantry during the Peninsular Campaign of the Napoleonic Wars 1804 - 1814.

NAPOLEON'S RUSSIAN CAMPAIGN by *Philippe Henri de Segur*—The Invasion, Battles and Retreat by an Aide-de-Camp on the Emperor's Staff

SWORDS OF HONOUR by *Henry Newbolt & Stanley L. Wood*—The Careers of Six Outstanding Officers from the Napoleonic Wars, the Wars for India and the American Civil War. Illustrated.

HUSSAR IN WINTER by *Alexander Gordon*—A British Cavalry Officer during the retreat to Corunna in the Peninsular campaign of the Napoleonic Wars.

THE LIFE OF THE REAL BRIGADIER GERARD VOLUME 1 THE YOUNG HUSSAR 1782 - 1807 by *Jean-Baptiste De Marbot*—A French Cavalryman Of the Napoleonic Wars at Marengo, Austerlitz, Jena, Eylau & Friedland.

THE LIFE OF THE REAL BRIGADIER GERARD VOLUME 2 IMPERIAL AIDE-DE-CAMP 1807 - 1811 by *Jean-Baptiste De Marbot*—A French Cavalryman of the Napoleonic Wars at Saragossa, Landshut, Eckmuhl, Ratisbon, Aspern-Essling, Wagram, Busaco & Torres Vedras.

THE LIFE OF THE REAL BRIGADIER GERARD VOLUME 3 COLONEL OF CHASSEURS 1811 - 1815 by *Jean-Baptiste De Marbot*—A French Cavalryman in the retreat from Moscow, Lutzen, Bautzen, Katzbach, Leipzig, Hanau & Waterloo.

RIFLEMAN COSTELLO by *Edward Costello*—The adventures of a soldier of the 95th (Rifles) in the Peninsular & Waterloo Campaigns of the Napoleonic wars.

WITH THE LIGHT DIVISION by *John H. Cooke*—The Experiences of an Officer of the 43rd Light Infantry in the Peninsula and South of France During the Napoleonic Wars.

COLBORNE: A SINGULAR TALENT FOR WAR by *John Colborne*—The Napoleonic Wars Career of One of Wellington's Most Highly Valued Officers in Egypt, Holland, Italy, the Peninsula and at Waterloo.

A VOICE FROM WATERLOO by *Edward Cotton*—The Personal Experiences of a British Cavalryman Who Became a Battlefield Guide and Authority on the Campaign of 1815.

AVAILABLE ONLINE AT
www.leonaur.com
AND OTHER GOOD BOOK STORES

www.ingramcontent.com/pod-product-compliance
Lightning Source LLC
Chambersburg PA
CBHW021010090426
42738CB00007B/732